S·U·P·E·R·C·A·R·S

LAMBORGHINI COUNTACH

BRIAN LABAN

a Salamander book

Published by Salamander Books Limited
LONDON • NEW YORK

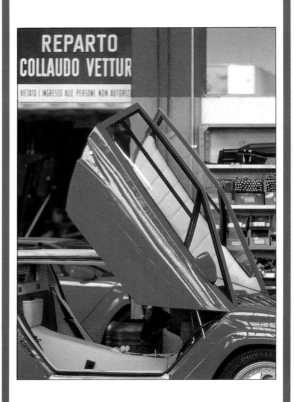

Contents

A SALAMANDER BOOK

Published by Salamander Books Ltd,
52 Bedford Row,
London WC1R 4LR

© Salamander Books Ltd, 1989

ISBN 0 86101 442 1

Distributed in the United Kingdom by
Hodder & Stoughton Services,
P.O. Box 6, Mill Road,
Dunton Green, Sevenoaks,
Kent TN13 2XX

Editor: Richard Collins

Designer: Paul Johnson

Line diagrams: Keith Palmar
(© Salamander Books Ltd)

Colour profile: Stephen Seymour
(© Salamander Books Ltd)

Filmset by Flair plan Photo-typesetting Ltd

Colour reproduction by Scantrans, Singapore

Printed in Italy

Acknowledgements
Thanks are due to many people for their help during the research for this book, most notably to president of Nuova Automobili Lamborghini, Emile Novaro, and to Daniele Audetto and Sandro Munari of the Lamborghini press office; to Nuccio Bertone and Marcello Gandini for sharing their insight and enthusiasm, and to Bertone press officer Dr Gian Beppe Panicco for bringing us together. Thanks to Mike Perry of Portman Lamborghini in the UK, and to Barry Robinson and Keith Downs, for opportunities to drive both Countachs and Miuras.

INTRODUCTION

In a world where motor manufacturers spend minor fortunes and years of soul-searching in arriving at a suitable name for even the most mundane of new models, the Countach is perhaps unique; the Countach virtually named itself.

The car that many think is the ultimate production supercar began life in the early 1970s at Lamborghini's impressive factory at Sant'Agata near Bologna, and at Bertone's Turin styling studios, as project number 112. Later, it became known as LP500, for *Longitudinale Posteriore* (longitudinal rear engine layout) and the 5-litre engine of the prototype. But when the first completed example was wheeled out of the workshops, legend has it that Nuccio Bertone himself took one look at the stunningly styled car and exclaimed, simply, 'Countach!'.

It is a local, Piedmontese dialect word for which there is no literal translation; but say it to yourself with the appropriate mixture of almost dumbstruck awe and amazement and you will understand. And so the LP500 became the Countach.

When it was first shown, as a prototype in 1971, the car-building part of the Lamborghini empire was barely eight years old, but it already had one major supercar, the Miura, to its credit. It was a young company with young engineers and a refreshingly open mind on new ideas. Many of the people who were involved in creating the Miura also helped give birth to the Countach, and this is also their story: of engineers Stanzani, Bizzarrini and Dallara; of works test driver Wallace; of Marcello Gandini, the man who styled both the Miura and Countach for Bertone;

and, of course, of Ferruccio Lamborghini himself.

Now, it is almost twenty years since the Countach was first conceived, and, while other supercars have come and gone, it remains one of the most stunning, uncompromising cars in the world – and still one of the fastest.

To stay ahead, it has changed dramatically, both aerodynamically and mechanically, and the story has not yet reached its conclusion; in 1988 the Anniversary Countach celebrated Lamborghini's twenty fifth anniversary as a supercar manufacturer, the company's future as part of the giant Chrysler group finally looks assured, and the next generation Countach, already being finalised as the Diablo, may well celebrate a quarter century for the model itself.

LAMBORGHINI – THE MAN

Ferruccio Lamborghini was born under the star sign of the bull. It became the symbol of his empire and determination

Y OU CAN COUNT THE RANKS of the surviving mainstream supercar makers comfortably on one hand: Aston Martin, Ferrari, Lamborghini and Porsche. Arguably, of those still in production, you could add De Tomaso on the strength of the past; you might add Maserati on the strength of *their* past and a frankly fading promise for the future; and perhaps you can throw in a few individual cars which have the performance and engineering integrity to be called supercar, but which in harsh reality will never really progress much beyond the one-off stage.

The *real* survivors are a very small élite indeed, and the one thing that characterises the leading triumvirate of Ferrari, Lamborghini and Porsche is that Enzo Ferrari, Ferruccio Lamborghini and Ferdinand Porsche were not only very successful car makers, but also very exceptional individuals.

Until his death in August 1988, Enzo Ferrari *was* Ferrari – even though the production side of his company was taken over by the giant Fiat conglomerate in 1969; and the Porsche dynasty which started with Professor Ferdinand's design skills in the early years of the century has continued with his son Ferry through the whole history of Porsche as a manufacturer, ever since the design consultancy turned to building cars under its own name in 1948.

And then there is Lamborghini. Like Ferrari, Lamborghini himself was forced by circumstance to sell his organisation to the big battalions, but, also like Ferrari, the empire would never have existed in the first place without his own vision and determination.

FERRUCCIO LAMBORGHINI
The man behind the name

Ferruccio Lamborghini was born on 28 April 1916, under the star sign of Taurus, which eventually gave his companies their raging bull emblem; many people would also say it gave him his direct and unswerving approach to life and particularly to business.

He was born the son of a farming family in the small rural village of Renazzo de Cento in the Ferrara district of northern Italy, within 20 miles or so of where both Ferrari and Adolfo Orsi, the industrialist who took over Maserati in the 1930s, were born. His parents were not large landowning farmers, but they made a reasonable enough living from their twenty acres or so, even around the lean years of World War I, and Ferruccio had a fairly comfortable upbringing.

His interest in farming was strictly limited; he was far more interested in motors and all things mechanical. As a young man, even before he moved from the farm to the city, he built himself a workshop of sorts in one of his father's farm buildings. And he took his interest in engineering seriously enough to equip his workshop with a forge from which he could produce fairly simple castings and forgings. He also, almost inevitably, managed to set fire to a number of the buildings he had taken over.

In that respect, his wasn't an especially unusual adolescence; Enzo Ferrari, born just eighteen years before Lamborghini, had been the son of a rural metalworker from nearby Modena, and, although he had had early aspirations as both opera singer and sports journalist, he soon gravitated back to the life of artisan; and Ferdinand Porsche was the third child of a tinsmith from Bohemia, who joined the family business from an early age, became interested first in electricity, and soon rigged up a workable electrical system for the family home and their small workshops.

Next step for Lamborghini was a more formal engineering education, and that is what his obviously understanding parents arranged for him. As soon as he was old enough he went to industrial college in Bologna, the Fratelli Taddia Institute. He graduated with a degree in industrial engineering and went to work part time in a motor repair workshop, also earning himself enough to buy a motor cycle, and dabble in a little two-wheeled racing. He raced both Gileras and Nortons, won his first race as the leader broke down, but readily admits he wasn't very good at it, and he crashed the Norton four times.

He was in his early twenties when World War II broke out and he found himself attached to a mechanical detachment of the Italian Air Force, working on vehicle maintenance on all manner of vehicles. He was eventually stationed at an air force base on the island of Rhodes, and obviously cultivated something of a reputation as an innovator. At some point he apparently suggested he could improve the cable braking system of the island governor's Alfa 1750 by adding an arrangement of springs into the cable runs to equalise the

Below: Sant'Agata Bolognese, the home of Automobili Lamborghini SpA, lies in the heart of the rich farmlands of the Emilia Romagna – a region well-known for its delicious food and fast cars – not far from Maranello and arch rivals Ferrari. Ferrari test their cars on their own track at Fiorano, Lamborghini on the road or in privacy at Nardo, in the south of Italy.

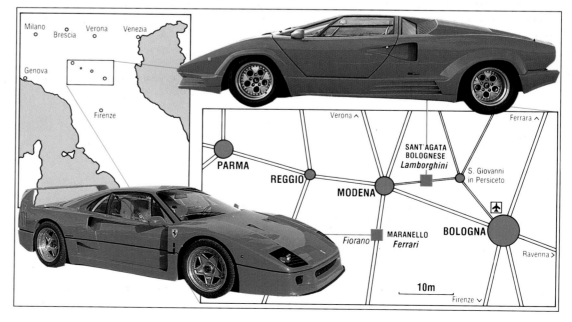

braking effort to each wheel. Testing the modifications himself, he put the car off the road and into the sea, without, it seems, either injury or recrimination.

When the Allies took Rhodes, Lamborghini was technically a prisoner of war but continued to work on Allied vehicles until 1946.

THE NEXT STEPS
A short, sharp career in racing!

From Rhodes he returned close to home, to Cento, where he went back to his small garage and tuning shop, specialising, predictably, in Fiats. For himself he modified a Fiat 500, increasing its capacity to 750cc and converting it from side to overhead valves. The cylinder head conversion he made was machined from bronze and gave the car the nickname *'Testa d'Oro'* (or 'golden head'). He built copies of the car for customers and raced his own example in the 1947 Mille Miglia, as car number 427, with a co-driver named Gian Luigi Baglioni, another farmer and a close friend. He completed about three quarters of the race before, according to his own version, crashing into the front of a bar. It was his first and last race on four wheels: 'that was enough racing for me,' he admitted many years later. 'I stayed and ordered a glass of vino . . .'

Around the same time he had found a profitable new business converting surplus military machinery into much needed tractors for the equipment starved post-war Italian farming industry. With his knowledge of Allied forces' hardware and impressed by their military equipment, he began with a batch of around fifty British Army surplus six-cylinder Morris engines, Ford gearboxes and narrowed General Motors back axles. By 1948 he was building more sophisticated tractors with many more of his own parts and in the same year he set up his first company, Lamborghini Trattori. The tractors were mostly painted yellow and carried the bull insignia.

Within three years, Lamborghini was building his own engines (all air-cooled) and gearboxes and expanding fast. In 1959, by which time he was building around ten tractors a day, he built two prototype helicopters, but he was refused a manufacturing licence by the government. So instead of building helicopters, he started the second element of his empire, manufacturing oil-fired heating equipment, and from 1960 air-conditioning equipment, as Lamborghini Bruciatori.

Others were in the manufacturing business before him, but Lamborghini realised that although the systems were easy and quite cheap to make, the real scope for commercial success lay in offering after-sales service to back up the product. He studied the competition, designed a better machine, and finally set up a countrywide, twenty-four-hours-a-day, seven-days-a-week servicing and maintenance organisation of some 2000 trained engineers.

BRANCHING OUT
The passion for fast cars

By the early 1960s, tractor output was up to twenty a day, Lamborghini was a wealthy man and, like many rich Italians, he could indulge a passion for fast cars, with 'a couple of Ferraris, a Mercedes, an American car; but I felt that I could do at least as well.'

The legend goes that Lamborghini had had cause to complain to Ferrari about recurring faults on one of his cars and had been summarily dismissed by the great Ferrari as a tractor maker who could know nothing of the niceties of super-

Above: Only two examples of Touring's stunning 350GT Spyder were ever made; the first was exhibited at the Turin Show in 1965.

Below left: The V12 engine in downdraught Weber carb form was not what Ferruccio had ordered and was soon toned down for the 350GT.

Below right: The father of the Lamborghini empire, Ferruccio Lamborghini. He was born into a farming family and, after he lost

control of his car and tractor companies in the 1970s, he returned to the land as a wine grower, near Panicarola, in central Italy.

car engineering. Apocryphal the story may be, but Lamborghini determined that if he couldn't *buy* a car good enough for his own demands he would build one himself – and for anyone else who wanted the best with no compromises.

In 1963 he founded Automobili Ferruccio Lamborghini SpA, investing millions of lire in a new factory at Sant'Agata Bolognese and in the engineering talent necessary to turn his ideas into reality. And while the factory was being built, the first car was already taking shape, piecemeal, in a corner of the tractor factory, already under the direction of the engineering team which would shape the future of the company: Bizzarrini, Dallara, Stanzani and Wallace.

The first car, with Bizzarrini's classic V12 engine (which is still the basis of today's Countach units), and chassis by Dallara, was shown in prototype form at the 1963 Turin Show. It was acclaimed for its engineering but few people liked the 2 + 2 coupé body styled by Franco Scaglione of Carrozzeria Sargiotto in Turin. When the car went into production in 1964 with a slightly less rabid version of the V12, it had an elegant new body by Touring and the designation 350GT. Although it appeared at a time when Italy was having one of the worst crises in its financial history, especially

in the car industry, it was extremely well received; it seems that the press were ready to welcome a new supercar maker.

ROCKING THE ESTABLISHMENT
The big ideas become reality

The national financial problems kept production figures well down on original intentions, but they began to climb quickly as the economy recovered and Lamborghini began to produce a steady stream of sensational production and show models. Some of the latter, like the Miura and the Countach, developed a habit of turning into the former, against all public expectations.

For Lamborghini, it seemed, nothing was impossible, and by 1967 there were distributors in Italy, the USA, Germany, Switzerland and Britain and Lamborghini were aiming at producing around 250 cars a year.

Yet the problems were never far away and by 1970 Ferruccio's companies were feeling the strains of the economic climate again, especially through Italian strikes and ever tougher US safety and emission regulations for the cars. Around this time the company was making a bid for the smaller sportscar market, with the Bertone-styled 2½-litre (152cu.in.) V8 Urraco, their first car built specifically to meet all US regulations, but that and the open-topped Silhouette derivative became victims of circumstance.

Lamborghini Trattori was very badly affected by a political crisis in Bolivia which caused the cancellation of an order for some 5000 tractors, at a time when the Italian economy was again experiencing one of its periodic downturns. To have any chance of saving the tractor operation, Lamborghini had no option but to sell a large part of his supercar company, and in 1970 he sold 51 per cent of the company to Swiss industrialist Georges-Henri Rossetti. Rossetti had intended to have a hands-on involvement in the company but a serious illness just after his acquisition left him in Switzerland while Ferruccio ran the company day to day as best he could with a controlling but inaccessible partner.

FORCED TO SELL
Ferruccio battered by financial problems
The situation continued to deteriorate and in 1972, finally beaten, Lamborghini sold his remaining shareholding to Réné Leimer, a Swiss associate of Rossetti's. After Ferruccio's departure things grew steadily worse. In 1976, Rossetti and Leimer appointed an ex-De Tomaso man, Pier Luigi Cappelini, to try to rescue the struggling company. In 1977 Cappelini and his associates arranged a deal which looked as though it would safeguard the company's future, signing an agreement with BMW to build 400 examples of their mid-engined M1 sports car for Group 4 racing and as a roadgoing supercar.

The catch was that, although the government had provided some funds on the strength of the BMW contract, some had gone to bail the company out of their immediate problems, and some had gone on the abortive off-road 'Cheetah' project (forerunner of today's LM cars) for the American Mobility Technology International company. When production of the M1 was due to start in July 1977, Lamborghini had to ask BMW themselves for help with the finance, BMW refused and the contract was withdrawn early in 1978. It was becoming a very complicated and worrying period for the company.

GOVERNMENT CONTROL
Surviving on the very brink
In August 1978 the government took control, and put in a receiver, Dr Allesandro Artese, to try and make something of the business. Artese did well to keep things going, albeit on a much reduced scale, and he eventually found the promise of support from a German financial group headed by Raymond Neumann. There was also a possibility at the time of a link with Canadian oil millionaire Walter Wolf, who sponsored the Wolf Grand Prix racing team and who was a longstanding Lamborghini customer.

In the end Wolf was denied the opportunity to buy into the company but what he did do was important to the future of the Countach, and that was to finance the development of the car (for his own use) around the new generation of ultra-low profile Pirelli tyres, the famous P7. Lamborghini first used the P7 on the Silhouette, as shown at Geneva in March 1976, and the Wolf-financed development led fairly directly to the Countach S, as launched in 1978.

The German connection was extended through a brief involvement by former BMW racer and German Lamborghini importer Hubert Hahne, who became general manager briefly from November 1979, but by 1980 the company was back

Above: Twin headlights distinguish the bigger engined 400GT, which soon followed on from the first Lamborghini production model, the 350GT. Dallara is on the right of this group, in spectacles, and test driver Bob Wallace is in the passenger's seat for once. *Below: The four-wheel-drive, off-road Cheetah, unveiled at the Geneva Show in March 1977, was built in San Jose, California, in* collaboration with Mobility Technology International. It used a Chrysler V8 and was the forerunner of the LM series; it came at a bad time.

under government auspices after the Germans had failed to come up with the promised funds.

SAVING THE COUNTACH
An image worth fighting for
In January 1979, however, one Giulio Alfieri had joined Lamborghini as a consultant, and after the German backing had evaporated Alfieri became general manager. Alfieri's credentials were impressive. He was a highly respected engineer fresh from a long and successful career with Maserati. His head-on approach, very much in the Ferruccio Lamborghini mould, was even more impressive. He looked at what the company had, at its assets and liabilities and he rationalized it. He dropped the Silhouette and the Urraco, turned the Jalpa into a production reality, and most of all

made it absolutely clear that the no-compromise Countach was the strongest single card in the company's depleted deck.

Complementary to Alfieri's wisdom was yet another new proprietor: the Mimram family. In July 1980 the court in Bologna relaxed the official grip on the company to the extent that the Mimrams (Swiss-based but with business interests mainly in Senegal) were allowed to lease the factory, with an option to buy. With Patrick Mimram as president, barely twenty-five years old but a very astute businessman and genuinely committed to making Lamborghini work, things improved. On 23 May 1981 the Mimram group exercised their option to purchase the company and Automobili Ferruccio Lamborghini SpA became Nuova Automobili Lamborghini.

Above: Lamborghini should have built the limited edition mid-engined M1 sports car for BMW in the late 1970s, but financial problems *prevented that from happening and took the company to the very brink of bankruptcy. The M1 had only a brief career in racing.*

ALFIERI'S CHALLENGE
Building a future around the Countach

It was the Mimrams who gave Alfieri the backing to save Lamborghini, and the Countach which gave him the hope that it could be done. His way ahead was clear: 'This factory had a car, the Countach, that offered the possibility of life. It was life without profit, but it was life – we had the possibility to save the workers and the suppliers. It was a challenge . . .'

And the challenge was met. Gradually things improved, the workforce grew again, the cars were constantly developed – especially the mighty Countach. It was never easy but the company was finally turned around to such an extent that it became attractive to big league predators once again, and in June 1987, after some eighteen months of negotiation, the giant Chrysler Corporation bought Lamborghini for around $30 million, some £12 million at the time.

Now, with the security of Chrysler backing but with the freedom to continue managing their own affairs, Lamborghini have a fascinating future. The company will expand, there will be new cars for different areas of the market, and there will very definitely be a successor to the Countach.

BACK TO THE LAND
Ferruccio never gives up

As for Ferruccio Lamborghini, the man who started it all, as well as selling his car company to Rossetti and Leimer, he sold his tractor business to Fiat in the early 1970s and used the proceeds to move back to the land.

For many years he had owned La Fiorata, an estate of some 750 acres near Panicarola in Umbria, central Italy, which he had originally seen just as hunting land. When he 'retired' he turned the estate into an arable farm, with almost 200

Above: The outwardly healthy look of the factory during the heyday of Miura production belied endless financial and labour *relations problems – which made it a minor miracle that the Countach ever happened at all. The Mimram family helped to stop the rot.*

acres of vineyards. He admits that he deeply regretted being forced to sell out of his other businesses, and especially his beloved cars, but he approached his return to farming in the same thorough way he approached every other business interest. He studied the needs and possibilities, invested heavily, built whatever it took – in this case a complete irrigation and road system for the whole area – and bought the very best vines for a wine to bear his own name.

He had legal battles with the Mimrams over his right to *use* his own name on non-automobile products, which has a certain irony. Now he has a

family villa (which, inevitably, he designed himself) at Casalecchio, in the hills overlooking Bologna, where he lives with his second wife, Patrizia. He stays fit and active, and nowadays when the sun shines he likes nothing better than to work on his farm.

There are constant rumours that he would one day love to build one more supercar, and he certainly keeps in touch with old associates and friends like Nuccio Bertone and some of the engineers, but money is always the problem. So, for now, it is his wines.

One of his impressive reds is called Sange di Miura: Bull's Blood. And the motto on the labels of his wine bottles reads *'Ho sempre cercato di fare il meglio in ogni campo. Questo è il mio vino'* – 'I have always tried to do my best in every sphere. This is my wine'.

DEVELOPING THE COUNTACH

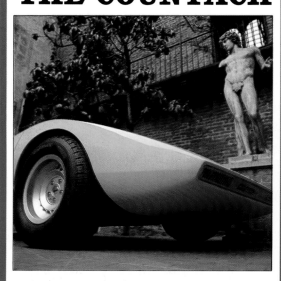

From prototype to final generation, the Countach has rarely stood still

WHEN THE PROTOTYPE Countach first appeared, on the Bertone stand at the Geneva Motor show in March 1971, it would have been so easy to have admired its stunning looks and remarkable engineering specification and then immediately dismiss it as simply another skin-deep beauty, cynically cobbled together by a specialist manufacturer and a flamboyant stylist. It looked sensational but it would surely never progress beyond being another non-running, impossible-to-build showstopper?

Anyone who did dismiss the LP500 so peremptorily would have been making a grave mistake.

THE MIURA
The Countach's spiritual forerunner
True enough, Lamborghini as a car company were barely eight years old; and, true enough, on their own stand at Geneva in 1971 they already had one of the most sensational production cars in the world. That was the Miura, introduced just five years earlier and shown here for the first time in what would turn out to be its final and most potent form – the 385bhp SV. Ironically, it was the Countach which killed the Miura.

Maybe the Countach prototype should have given the cynics pause for thought. After all, Lamborghini had made quite a habit of launching new cars into the public gaze in Geneva. In 1964, the giant Palexpo halls had seen the debut of their very first production car, the 350GT; in 1967 they had unveiled the Marzal; in 1968 it was the Islero and the Espada; in 1970 the Jarama. Of those, only the glass-sided, six-cylinder Marzal failed to make the transition into production.

And the Miura (in effect only the second distinct model Lamborghini had built, and the Countach's spiritual forerunner) had also started its life as a production car in the same show hall in Geneva, in 1966.

Only a few months earlier, at the Turin Show in November 1965, the Miura had been seen as even more of a show car than the Countach was in 1971. It appeared first as nothing more than an unclothed rolling chassis with a revolutionary transverse mid-engine layout. Anyone who thought it had any future purpose at all naturally assumed that it was the thin end of the racing wedge for Lamborghini.

It wasn't, and just those few months later the Miura appeared again, but this time spectacularly clothed by Bertone as a roadgoing mid-engined two-seater which made any other contemporary production car look primitive.

That, remember, was 1966, and the Miura's supercar contemporaries were front-engined cars like the Ferrari 330GT 2+2 and the 275GTB/4. It was two years before Ferrari introduced the Daytona, a sensational car in its own right, but technically from a previous generation, still with the front engine layout and square rigged conventionality. It was a year before Ferrari would wheel out the first roadgoing mid-engined Dino, and this was seven years ahead of their larger, mid-engined Boxer. If the Miura had a real contemporary cousin, it was not any road car but the Le Mans winning Ford GT40 racer.

1971: LAMBORGHINI, BERTONE . . .
. . . and their futuristic supercar
And now, in 1971, Lamborghini and Bertone were doing it all over again with this incredible device called the Countach, another mid-engined two-seater supercar, but this time with styling so futuristic, and technical solutions so brilliant, that it made even the Miura seem almost ordinary.

It was so typically Lamborghini to produce a car like the Countach just as the vultures were gathering to pick clean the bones of what they saw as a dying company; but there was to be no 'I

told you so' fate for what many still regarded as an upstart among the old guard – even though times in the early 1970s were desperately bad at Sant'Agata.

In many ways, the prototype Countach reflected exactly what it was that had helped Lamborghini succeed: it showed a genuinely fresh way of thinking, a sense of adventure, and above all the open-mindedness of a young company – not yet stifled by old-guard tradition but still with everything to prove.

As the Countach appeared on the Bertone stand at Geneva in March 1971 (as the LP500), it was recognisably the Countach of today, even though virtually every aspect has changed dramatically in the years since. And in its bright yellow paintwork and with very little adornment, it was not just a non-running mock-up (as so many show cars are), but a complete, drivable vehicle. It had been hastily completed just days before, and actually *driven* at least part of the way from Sant'Agata to the show by test driver Bob Wallace.

A very different car from the Miura, it shared the mid-engined, two-seater sports configuration, but that was about all. The big difference under the futuristic skin was revealed by the type number: LP500.

DALLARA AND THE MIURA
Refining the transverse mounted engine

The Miura had been launched as the TP400, where 400 stood for the V12 engine's 4-litre (244cu. in.) capacity and where TP signified the engine position: *Transversale Posteriore*, or rear, transverse mounted. At the time, that had been a typically brave and unfettered engineering decision by Giampaolo Dallara, the young engineer who designed the Miura. Not only had he admired the racing GT40 for its whole concept, but he had also been deeply impressed by Alec Issigonis's slightly more humble Mini. The Mini was still only a few years old (launched in 1959) and the idea of a transverse engine with its gearbox and final drive in the sump was still quite revolutionary.

In the Mini's case, Issigonis had conceived the layout to allow him to build a compact, front-wheel-drive saloon. Dallara saw no reason why that should not be equally practicable with a rear-drive sports car. With the open-mindedness of the great engineer, he apparently saw no insurmountable difference between the original Mini's layout with a mass-produced four-cylinder, 37bhp pushrod, single-carburettor engine, and the Miura's thoroughbred, four-cam, six twin-choke carburettored 350bhp V12.

It worked, up to a point, but the Miura did have its problems.

The transverse layout kept the length of the car to not only reasonable but also absolutely beautiful proportions. The effect of 350bhp and 8000rpm churning the heavyweight gear cluster directly in the sump, though, had predictably deleterious effects on the lubricating oil; that meant that the Miura had to be looked after very carefully indeed if it was to enjoy any kind of longevity. The gear linkage too was problematical with this layout, and routine access was a nightmare.

Aside from that, the Miura did have some problems with high speed directional stability because of the relationship between its tail-heavy weight distribution and nose-light aerodynamic properties. They were especially manifest in a tendency for the front end to try to lift at very high speeds.

It was a great car, but it *was* flawed.

The whole concept of the Countach, or more properly the LP500 as it was known at that stage, was to extend the Miura's ethos as *the* state-of-the-art roadgoing sports car, and to make it more refined and more usable.

FERRUCCIO'S CHALLENGE
Throwing down the gauntlet to Ferrari

Ferruccio Lamborghini wanted the Countach to be unique; a car with near racing performance (both in speed and handling) but also with true grand touring ambience. He wanted it to outperform any conceivable rival – and that really meant Ferrari – but he also wanted it to be the sort of car any wealthy, discriminating enthusiast could drive over long distances with a high degree of comfort, practicality and dependability. In short, he wanted it to be everything he had always wanted all his cars to be from the moment he decided to attack his great Maranello rival, but in this case he wanted it to be so to the ultimate degree.

At the same time as he wanted it to be the ultimate prestige car, though, he *didn't* want it simply to be a flippant status symbol. He was very serious about the Countach's worth, and he wasn't about to compromise its engineering simply to make a rich man's toy . . .

The key to the Countach's differences over the hugely successful Miura was to be seen in that new designation, LP500. Now (for the first concept at least), the 500 stood for a full 5-litre (305 cu.in.) engine and the LP signified not a *transversale* engine but *Longitudinale Posteriore*: rear, longitudinally mounted.

LP500: THE NEW CONCEPT
Developing the longitudinally mounted engine

The problem of accommodating the long V12 engine, its gearbox and final drive, in the middle of a two-seater car, hadn't gone away since Dallara adopted the transverse engine, gears-in-sump solution; but Dallara himself had left the company

Below: Gandini's styling for the Miura owed more to then-current racing designs such as the GT40 than to other road cars. Air intakes were a visual device to tie together top and bottom styling elements.

in August 1968, frustrated by Lamborghini's continuing refusal to go racing, and the appointment of a new chief engineer.

The new chief engineer was Paolo Stanzani, originally Dallara's assistant, and Stanzani had thought of a new and perhaps even more elegant solution to the mid-engined problem. What he did with the layout is really the heart of the Countach; he turned the big V12 engine through 90°, to run along the length of the chassis rather than being mounted across it.

That in itself was not unusual; several cars now had this 'mid-engined' configuration, where the engine and gearbox were behind the driver but ahead of the rear axle line; it had even been done with V12 engines in racing cars.

'Conventionally', though, the engine was placed at the front of the assembly, driving back through the gearbox and a final drive located behind it. With smaller engines that was reasonably workable, but with something the size of the Lamborghini V12 it would have pushed the passenger compartment unfeasibly far forward, or made the car overall impractically large.

ENGINEERING GENIUS
Stanzani's unique engine layout

Stanzani's remarkable innovation was to turn the engine around so that the gearbox was in front of it, effectively located between the driver and passenger, where its relative narrowness allowed it to fit quite comfortably. He then took the drive *back* from the gearbox output, via a shaft running in a sealed tube within the engine's sump, to a final drive unit at the rear end of the engine (nominally the front in normal terms!) also within the sump casting, and thence to the rear wheels.

Like all the best ideas it is essentially very simple and at a stroke it overcame many of the Miura's problems. It made the Countach a better balanced car; the gear lever acted directly into the box without the Miura's serpentine and often baulky linkage; and it separated the engine lubrication from the gearbox lubrication (which the Miura itself had finally been obliged to do in the 385bhp SV).

And, amazingly, the Countach with its longitudinal engine was actually shorter in both wheelbase and overall length than the Miura with its transverse set-up.

That unique layout apart, the LP500 Countach as it first appeared was mechanically fairly conventional. Although the Countach concept had been kicking around since probably 1969, the car had finally been built in the usual last-minute rush to make that March 1971 Geneva debut.

The chassis of the prototype was described by Lamborghini as a 'monocoque', but in reality it was a fairly simple steel spaceframe with welded on panels, and it used mainly square section tubing. The suspension was obviously fully independent, with double wishbones, coil springs and telescopic dampers all round, and with anti-roll bars at each end, and it was based almost entirely on production parts. The chassis used Girling ventilated disc brakes all round, with a dual hydraulic system and twin servos. It was relatively basic by Lamborghini's production car standards, but it got the show on the road.

The 5-litre (305cu.in.) engine was unique to this car. Lamborghini, in truth, still wasn't really committed to building the Countach as a production model, but even a show car has to come up with some big numbers if it is to have the desired effect on the onlooker.

The motor was based on the existing production

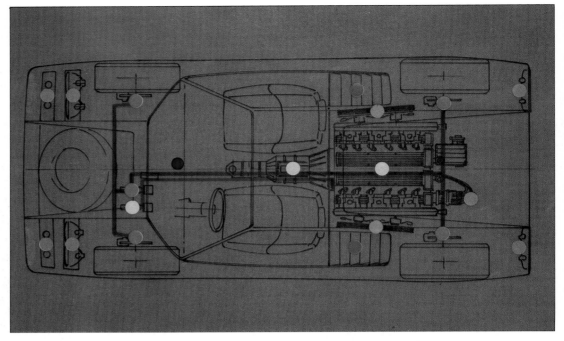

Above: Bertone's 'car-map' warning light drawing for the LP500 prototype's dash shows essential layout of the Countach. Stanzani's unique 'back-to-front' engine and transmission layout puts the gearbox ahead of the engine, and between driver and passenger. Final drive is at rear of engine, with short driveshafts to rear wheels. Original flush-mounted cooling ducts are featured in this early drawing, with radiators almost parallel to the engine, and marked here by the orange dots which would have been the cooling system warning lights. *Below: The LP500 show car soon became Wallace's test hack – and the futuristic dash already had an analogue speedometer buried in it by the time this picture was taken. Look closely at the standard of finish and it's not difficult to see that the car was built in a rush.* *Bottom left and right: The transverse-engined Miura layout that Stanzani rethought for the Countach was an ingenious solution, at least in terms of packaging, but what worked well for the small-engined Mini had practical problems when translated to a V12 supercar.*

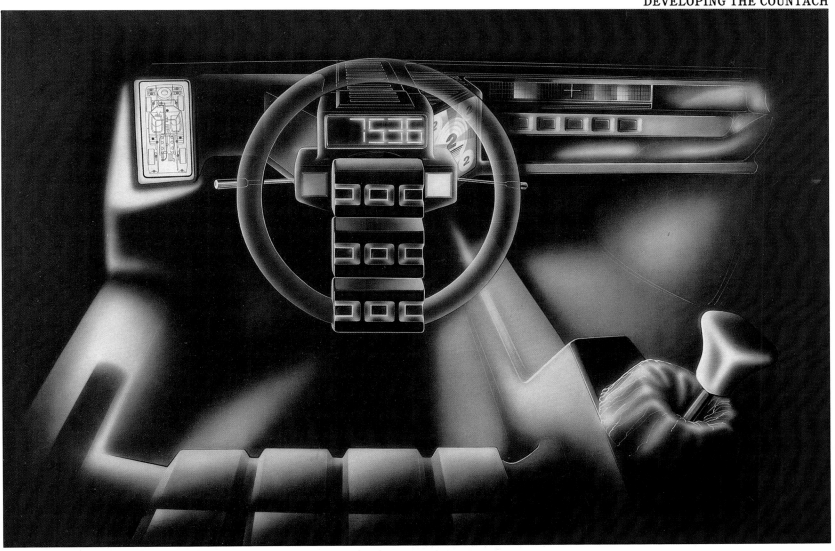

Above: Early styling drawing for the LP500 dash shows the digital and electronic approach that Bertone first had in mind for Gandini's futuristic creation. The car map warning system is to left of binnacle; rest of layout is simple and at this stage purely for styling. Block seats and steering wheel actually carried on to first prototype, but interior was altogether more conventional by the time production started.

Below: The first LP500 prototype was the smoothest that Gandini's Countach shape would ever be, with the original high-downforce nose profile featuring a low leading edge and recessed central cover. This version also has the flush cooling duct arrangement, and the rear-view 'periscope' at the front of the roof tunnel. The nose, the cooling ducts and the roof were all changed before production.

V12, which at that stage had bore and stroke measurements of 3.23 × 2.44in. (82.0 × 62.0 mm), for a capacity of 3929cc (240cu.in.). In the Miura SV that was good for 385bhp at 7850rpm and 286lb ft of torque at 5000rpm. For the LP500, the dimensions were increased to 3.35 × 2.88in. (85.0 × 73.0mm) or 4971cc (303cu.in.); the compression ratio was a very high 11.5:1 and there were six twin-choke sidedraught Weber carbs. In that form, Lamborghini reported 440bhp at 7400rpm and a massive 366lb ft of torque at 5000rpm; in reality, the production Countach wouldn't better those figures until the 5000S *quattrovalvole* was launched, with 455bhp, in March 1985!

With that much power, Lamborghini claimed a maximum speed of 186mph (300kph) for the car, comfortably faster than Ferrari's contemporary rival, the front-engined 175mph (282kph) Daytona – if the LP500's claims were true.

Of course, at that stage, it didn't matter too much whether the speed was real or not; it wasn't just the big numbers that made the Countach spectacular, it was the way it looked too.

BERTONE AND STYLING
Enter Gandini

With the Miura, Lamborghini had begun a long association with Nuccio Bertone, head of the great styling house that bore his name, and in many ways a man much after Lamborghini's heart, with little time for long, drawn-out schemes. That had certainly been dramatically shown in the Miura's mere three-month styling gestation, and it was about to happen again with the Countach.

The same, brilliant stylist, Marcello Gandini, penned both cars.

Gandini has often been called a genius, and his genius started young. The Miura was literally his first styling job for Bertone, who he joined in 1965 as chief stylist, replacing the more famous Giorgetto Giugiaro, who was about to launch his own independent studio. Gandini was just twenty-seven when he joined Bertone, and he might have joined even earlier, but legend has it that Giugiaro wasn't too keen to have to compete with the obviously exceptional newcomer.

Whatever the politics, the association between Lamborghini and Bertone was firmly cemented by the Miura, and that was a weight off Ferruccio's mind; Ferrari had Pininfarina, Lamborghini *needed* a working relationship with a top line studio – and now he had it.

Between the Miura and the Countach, Gandini had drawn several other Lamborghini models – the Marzal, the Urraco, the Bravo and the Espada – but the real forerunner of the Countach if there was such a thing was a Gandini-styled Alfa Romeo show car of 1968, the Caràbo, whose name (the Italian version of Scarab) came from its colouring and the way its vertical door opening suggested a beetle's wing cases.

GANDINI AND THE COUNTACH
'Clean-sheet thinking at its best'

But at the end of the day, Gandini's styling for the Countach was clean-sheet thinking at its very best. Gandini will admit that there is a little bit of the Lola T70 sports racing car in the overall proportions of the Countach, but so far as external automotive influences go that is very much the sum of it. The Countach is more about form and the use of surfaces than it is about simply clothing a mechanical chassis. And in its earliest form as the 1971 show car, it demonstrates that purity of line in a much better manner than any subsequent

Below and right: Nuccio Bertone was the stylist that Ferruccio Lamborghini badly needed to find in the early days of his car company. The association started with the Miura and, although it was highly successful, it was hardly conventional by normal standards. Bertone and Lamborghini simply had a gentlemen's agreement...

Left and below: Marcello Gandini styled both the Countach and the Miura in his days at Bertone, as well as many other exceptional cars. Now he works from his own studio, outside Turin, and from here he penned the Countach's 1990s successor; whether all his ideas survive the new regime's changes remains to be seen.

production version of the car ever would.

Compromises for practicality are the difference. As the first, bright yellow LP500 appeared in Geneva, it was incredibly dramatic in the context of other models of the time, but it was really a very clean and simple shape. All the subsequent addenda – air scoops, ducts, wings, wheelarches and spoilers – have made the Countach more aggressive (and Gandini actually approves of that) but all the real drama of the shape was there from day one.

Look at the first show car: the proportions emphasise the power of the mid-mounted V12 without ever allowing you to see it; the wheelarch cutouts emphasise the size of the wheels needed to cope with the power; the look is smooth and slab-sided, but at the same time angular and menacing, hinting at the forward crouch of the predator; and the lozenge shaped, pontoon-like side elements are simply unique touches which maybe suggest some futuristic technology but in such a subliminal way as to be anything but corny. Stand the Countach today against most of the other 'futuristic' show cars of the early 1970s and you will see just how crass crystal-gazing can be without the genius of a Gandini . . .

And then there are the still unique doors. Just as on the Carabo, they open forwards and up, counterbalanced, hingeing on their leading edges and staying parallel to the sides of the car as they open. It is a styling touch, unashamedly, but it is also a practical solution to providing adequate access on a car which is already so wide that conventional openings, or even gullwings, would restrict the places where you could climb in or out of a Countach.

The LP500 was unquestionably a show car, but if there was any way of turning it into a production reality, there were people at Lamborghini who were absolutely determined to do it.

FROM SHOW CAR TO REALITY
Stanzani and Wallace get to work

Foremost among them were designer Stanzani and chief test driver Bob Wallace, a brilliant, highly experienced but genuinely modest New Zealander, with a racing team background at both Maserati and Ferrari. Wallace had joined Lamborghini right from the start and it had always been his talent and constant testing which made the clever engineering answers work on a practical, production level.

Almost as soon as the doors closed on the Geneva Show, Wallace started developing the LP500. The basis was actually better than anyone had expected, and even the hack show chassis proved quite drivable, with surprisingly good weight distribution thanks to Stanzani's clever drivetrain layout.

Wallace began testing the car both on the roads around Bologna and on various circuits, often with Stanzani or his assistant Massimo Parenti working the measuring equipment. Among the few things that were really troublesome in the early, 1971 tests was the 5-litre (305cu.in.) engine. Stanzani toyed with the possibilities of a 4.4-litre (268cu.in.) unit, but that line of development didn't go far, and it wasn't long before the test car was given a much more standard 4-litre (244cu. in.) unit. By this time, with some fairly long runs successfully completed by the prototype, and with a very positive reaction from putative buyers, the Countach's move into production was pretty well guaranteed but there were enough immediate problems to solve without having to develop the new engine too.

Above: The rear view of the LP500 prototype was even more dramatic than that of the front, clearly showing the geometric profile of the pontoon sides and Gandini's original intentions for the rear light shapes. They were another victim on the road to production.

Below: The dramatic Carabo, styled by Bertone and Gandini for Alfa Romeo in 1968, was in many ways the real starting point for the Countach – most obviously in the vertically hingeing door layout which gave the Countach its most spectacular styling trick.

At least the new shape was aerodynamically fairly sound right from the beginning, although the only real testing had been done with scale models in the Turin Polytechnic's wind tunnel. Wallace and Stanzani also carried out some suck-it-and-see testing with wool tufts on the bodywork on the road and the track, but generally the car was proving stable at high speeds and so remained virtually unchanged in that respect.

Mechanically, the biggest problem was over-heating, even with the smaller engine. The original layout had used horizontal radiators alongside the engine and louvred ducts set into the rear quarters of the car, flush with the surface, but these quickly showed up as hopelessly inadequate and the next pre-production cars had sprouted air scoops behind the doors and NACA ducts in the doors (into which the catches were set). The air was allowed out through slatted grilles on top of the originally smooth rear flanks.

What might have sounded like a compromise was coincidentally beginning to make the sleek Countach look steadily more aggressive and people seemed to like that.

TOWARDS A PRODUCTION CAR
Stanzani's sophisticated chassis

The 'periscope' rear view mirror in the roof was dropped between show car and pre-production models (although the 'tunnel' remained), the rear light shapes were revised slightly, and so were the nose shape, the front grille and the exhaust layout. Several rather ugly options were explored for giving the production cars the essential wind-screen wiper, an accessory which the show car had conveniently ignored.

There was another very major change under the skin, too, a much more sophisticated chassis, which looked incredibly complex but which satisfied all Stanzani's criteria. It had to be light, immensely rigid (to provide a stable platform for the suspension), strong in the event of an impact, and capable of being maintained and even repaired if the need arose.

The chassis which he designed (and which is essentially unchanged today) satisfied all those requirements and was clothed in a non-stressed light alloy body (to Bertone's specifications but fitted at the Sant'Agata factory).

When the car appeared again, at Geneva in 1973, it was well on its way towards a production specification, with conventional instruments replacing the original digital system, with some of the castings changed from magnesium to aluminium for practicality, and with all the other improvements that had been worked out up to that point. By that time, the delays were probably more financial and political than practical: the energy crisis was deepening, statutory requirements for cars were becoming more stringent, the financial and labour relations problems at the factory were dragging on, and, frankly, it was a miracle that the Countach ever happened at all . . .

But happen it did, and eventually, at Geneva in March 1974, it appeared as a fully fledged production model, the LP400.

GENEVA 1974
Prototype becomes production: the LP400

Two pre-production cars had been built, the original prototype was to be sacrificed to the obligatory barrier impact test for type approval in Britain in March 1974, and building in series began very late in 1973. Sadly, the arrival of the Countach would more or less coincide with the final departure of Ferruccio Lamborghini himself.

Above: The only time the Countach went near a wind tunnel was as a scale model, seen here in very early guise undergoing an ink-spot test in Turin Polytechnic's tunnel. Fortunately, the car was aerodynamically sound from the start, and a big improvement on the Miura.

Below: By the time the Countach reached production as the LP400, the look had changed quite markedly, and the feel was even more dramatic. The air scoops and NACA ducts added a touch of menace to the softer, feline lines of the uncluttered original.

Like the original prototype, the first 'production' car to be shown was yellow, in this case with a leather and suede interior, the dark suede being a clever way to cut down interior reflections, which could be a major problem with the big, steeply sloping screen (now swept by a huge, twin-bladed pantographic wiper).

The Countach now had the 3929cc (240cu. in.) four-cam V12 engine, with a 10.5:1 compression ratio and six twin-choke sidedraught Weber 45DCOE carburettors. It gave 375bhp at 8000rpm and 266lb ft of torque at 5000rpm. That drove through a five-speed Lamborghini gearbox and Stanzani's unique driveline to a ZF limited-slip differential (the prototype had used Lamborghini's own differential, but the ZF was always the production unit). The wheels were 15-inch diameter, 9½ inches wide at the rear and 7½ inches at the front (380 × 240 × 190mm), with Michelin XWX tyres, which were low profile for their day but now look very tall and round shouldered.

COUNTACH EVOLUTION CONTINUES
. . . with the Pirelli P7

That tyre configuration would be one of the first things to change in the Countach's continuous and steady evolution. At more or less the same time as the first production Countach appeared in 1974 on its 70 per cent profile Michelin tyres (the profile is the ratio of the sidewall height to the tread width), Pirelli were introducing a tyre which would revolutionise not just the tyre world but also suspension design across the board, and even the way cars looked. This was the now famous P7; it appeared first as original equipment on the Ferrari-engined Lancia Stratos rally car (coincidentally, another Gandini design) and its ultra-low, 50 per cent profile was only the most visible

construction industry. In 1967 he became a Canadian citizen and in 1968 he moved his interests into the oil exploration servicing industries. By the mid-1970s he was a multi-millionaire and his name became famous as patron of the Wolf Grand Prix racing team.

His first contact with Grand Prix racing was with the Williams team, who had recently been running De Tomaso Grand Prix cars, designed by none other than Giampaolo Dallara, who had gone to De Tomaso from Lamborghini in 1968 as a way of exorcising his craving for some racing activity. Early in 1975 Dallara had gone *back* to Lamborghini after Stanzani, progenitor of the Countach, left (as did Wallace), in the wake of all the commercial upheavals.

For a while, there was the possibility that Wolf might have bought out Lamborghini, and in the end, although he didn't actually buy the ailing company, his love of the Countach (which he liked to personalise to his own tastes) played a more important part in saving Lamborghini than most people realise. What Wolf did, purely for his own entertainment at first, was to bring together the Countach and the P7, and to make the combination work.

It marked the start of a 'second generation' Countach, at a time when the factory couldn't possibly have done it themselves.

Demand for the Countach was still there, in spite of appalling economic and worldwide energy problems, and there was always a steady stream of customers for the car, which was initially being built at the rate of about one a week, but there was no market at all for lesser Lamborghinis, and that meant no money. If the Countach hadn't survived, Lamborghini wouldn't have survived; it was that simple.

1978: THE LP400 S
Building on Wolf's lead

Yet, building on the lead given by Wolf, in 1978 Lamborghini were able to launch the Countach LP400 S, and the biggest difference was that the new car sat on Pirelli P7 tyres, with suspension modifications to match.

As well as the work done by Wolf on his own Countachs, the factory had gained some experience with the P7 on the smaller Silhouette (fore-runner of today's Jalpa), which they showed at Geneva (inevitably) in 1976. To make the Countach work on its new and spectacularly larger rubber, the location points for the springs and dampers had been relocated to decrease the geometry changes as the suspension did its work, new hubs and suspension uprights had been designed, a new anti-roll bar had been fitted at the front end and the steering rack had been revised. And at the rear, the suspension changed to two sets of twin parallel links with bigger hub bearings to cope with the increased loads. The tyres themselves were 205/50VR15s on the front, and a staggeringly wide and low 345/35VR15 on the rear, the 35 representing the lowest profile of any production tyre built.

There were other changes too. The original Girling brakes were replaced by ATE units, which used larger discs with racing-type four-pot calipers, to take advantage of the bigger tyre 'foot-print' offered by the P7s. And, most obviously, the body changed, with a new front spoiler, a rear

reason for its exceptional capabilities. The lower profile gave better control of the tread and so improved the distribution of loads across the whole contact patch, thus improving both ultimate grip and control, in acceleration and braking as well as in cornering. Yet at the same time, the P7 retained a flexibility and ride comfort that even the 'low-profile' 70-series types had to a large extent to sacrifice.

It was immediately obvious to any high-performance car manufacturer that the P7 was the key to dramatic new areas of chassis performance, but it wasn't quite so simple as just fitting the new tyres on to wide new wheels and bolting the whole lot to the car. The essence of a tyre like the P7 is that the suspension must be capable of exploiting the grip that it offers, essentially by controlling the angles to which it rolls and keeping the contact patch as flat as is necessary, all

while retaining both ride comfort and stability.

Even now that can be a very expensive science; when the first P7s appeared it was, necessarily, an even more experimental 'black-art', and in the early 1970s Lamborghini just didn't have the sort of resources to do the necessary work.

Fortunately for the future of the Countach, though, they had a customer who did have the resources, and the enthusiasm: Walter Wolf.

MID-SEVENTIES BLUES
Wolf to the rescue

Walter Wolf was born in Austria in 1939, moved to Germany in 1955 as an apprentice mechanic in an aircraft factory, and emigrated to America in 1959 with a private pilot's licence as his main asset. In 1960, virtually broke after working as a crop-duster pilot, he moved to Canada and within a few years he had built a sizeable business in the wing similar to that which Walter Wolf had contrived for his own cars – plus wider, glassfibre wheelarches to accommodate the bigger wheels and tyres.

It all combined to give the Countach the modern, chunky and aggressive look which is still obvious today.

Perversely, the LP400 S was one of the least successful Countachs, selling only 237 examples between 1978 and 1982, but that probably reflected the fact that Ferrari were at last catching up on Lamborghini (with the mid-engined Boxer, launched in 1974 and uprated to 5 litres in 1976), that the future of Lamborghini continued to be uncertain, and, unfortunately, that the outright ability of the Countach was slipping a little.

The new tyres, ironically, were partly to blame; their increased size and the aerodynamic penalty of covering them had sapped a little speed, and a slight softening of the engine for better drivability would gradually erode the power over the next couple of years and make the problem even worse. Of necessity, the LP400 S survived with nothing more than new style wheels and a revised dashboard with bigger instruments, all added in 1979. But it was obvious that something more fundamental was needed, and soon, to restore the Countach's status.

FERRARI BITE BACK
Lamborghini search for more power

One obvious problem was that the rival Boxer was a full 5 litres while the Countach was still only a 4.4 and, by September 1980, Lamborghini had made the decision that, whatever the company's problems, they had to find more power and torque, reduce specific fuel consumption and yet still keep the drivability which they had now built in.

In 1979 they had shown a turbocharged Countach design exercise at Geneva, but in reality it was not much more than a mock-up and (especially as it instantly antagonised the age old cooling problem even further) it was shelved fairly quickly. Instead, in 1982, Lamborghini first went the classic route of increasing engine capacity.

The V12 didn't quite go to the Boxer's full 5 litres (although the new model was called the LP500 S) but to 4754cc (290cu. in.), thanks to an increase in bore from 3.23 to 3.37in. (82.0 – 85.5mm) and an increase in stroke from 2.44 to 2.72in. (62.0 – 69.0mm).

The engine was generally beefed up to suit, the combustion chambers were redesigned, with a much lower compression ratio (down from 10.5 to 9.2:1) to give less sensitivity to lower octane fuels, the cams were revised and larger Weber 45DCOE sidedraught carbs were fitted. The result was more power, back up to the genuine 375bhp from which it had slipped backwards to 353bhp, and better flexibility: the power peak was now at 7000rpm rather than 7500 (or the 8000 of the earlier 375bhp unit) and the torque peak improved from the LP400 S's 266lb ft at 5500rpm to 303lb ft at a slightly more comfortable 4500rpm, with a rather better spread to boot. The gearing was changed too, with a slightly higher overall top gear – better to exploit the new power characteristics. Although the new car was slightly heavier, it was also usefully quicker.

Elsewhere, the Countach had already had further minor changes in adopting its LP400 S guise, with the floor raised slightly to give a more comfortable driving position, and the roof 'tunnel' (a legacy of the original periscope mirror) also disappearing on the S. The only real external changes on the LP500 S, though, were different

Right and above: Giulio Alfieri, with backing from the Mimram family, kept Lamborghini alive in the early 1980s. Alfieri saw the importance of the Countach and engineered the latest generation quattrovalvole engine, first seen in the version of the car, above.

badges, which actually said 5000.

The 500 S arrested the sales decline and restored the Countach's credibility as pre-eminent supercar, but Lamborghini already knew that the competition was getting tougher, especially as Ferrari were soon fighting back with the excellent 390bhp, 180mph (290kph) Testarossa, launched in 1984. There had to be more to come from the Countach.

It came with a vengeance at Geneva in March 1985, when Lamborghini launched the 5000 *quattrovalvole*.

BACK WITH A VENGEANCE
Alfieri and the 5000 *quattrovalvole*

The company now had more than its usual level of financial security since the Mimrams had taken the reins in 1980, and a brilliant engineer in the person of Giulio Alfieri, the new general manager. Alfieri had realised that without the Countach Lamborghini was dead and it was he who engineered the vastly improved new generation V12. With this superb new engine, they had not only raised capacity to a full 5 litres – to 5167cc (315cu. in.), in fact, by increasing the stroke from 2.72 to 2.95in. (69.0 – 75.0mm) – but also added four-valve *(quattrovalvole)* cylinder heads.

Four valves per cylinder (as opposed to the standard two) is a classical way of improving engine power without resorting to turbocharging or supercharging, and a more archetypally Italian way of doing things. Alfieri started the programme

late in 1984, aiming for 450bhp and cleaner exhaust emissions. The cylinder heads were obviously completely new, with straighter inlet tracts and downdraught carburettors to take full advantage of the valve layout, and the compression ratio went up again, to 9.5:1. On an early testbed trial Alfieri's new engine gave as much as 480bhp and, even when it was announced for production, the jump was very substantial – from 375bhp up to no less than 455bhp at 7000rpm, and a massive 369lb ft of torque at 5200rpm.

At a stroke, it took the Countach once again out of the reach of Ferrari's 390bhp Testarossa, and even their 'limited edition' GTO's 400bhp.

On top of the engine mods, the Countach gained slightly wider front tyres (still the famous P7s) with minor suspension geometry changes to match, and it gained a new engine cover with a large hump to cover the taller carbs. As with all the previous body modifications, it seemed to serve mainly to make the Countach look still more aggressive.

So far as engine and mechanical changes are concerned, that pretty well marks the end of the evolution of the classic Countach. Late in 1987, the bodywork was given further revisions, with

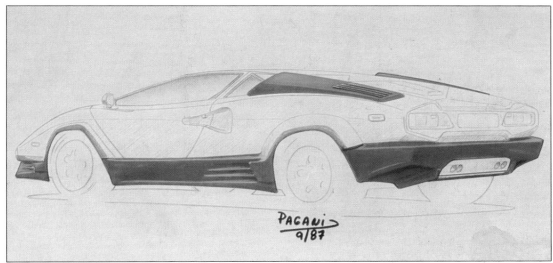

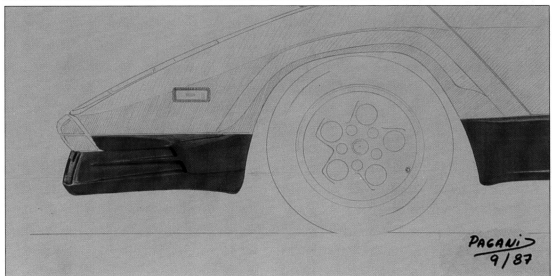

new straked sills incorporating functional brake cooling vents. Inside, it gained central locking, new heater controls and better ventilation, and under the skin it had the usual steady development of anything that moved, but nothing terribly dramatic – and certainly nothing reflecting the experiments which had been going on with a so-called 'super Countach' since mid-1985. All that is for the future.

TWENTY-FIVE YEARS
Celebrating with style

Finally, so far as the production life of the 'first generation' Countach goes, 1988 brought the 25th Anniversary car – celebrating the first quarter century for a company which has not only survived, seemingly against all the odds, but has also produced some of the most spectacular supercars of all.

The final Countach has substantially revised body styling, with much smoother lines around the massive rear cooling scoops, neater front and rear treatments (the former at last incorporating a universally acceptable bumper design where previous cars had to have an ugly add-on unit for the US market) and distinctive new wheels with a new generation of Pirelli tyre, the P Zero. There are new seats, a better air conditioning system, more sound insulation and the tiny 'toll-booth' side windows have finally gained electric operation.

Beneath the skin, though, things are largely unchanged apart from the inevitable suspension changes and some tinkering with the cooling system to suit the new bodywork. Any thoughts that the added creature comforts are a sign that the Countach is going soft in its middle age can be instantly dispelled simply by looking into the engine bay, where the fabulous four-valve V12 will now see the Countach through to its expected 1990s replacement. That Lamborghini is celebrating a 25th anniversary at all is quite remarkable; that they are celebrating it with the Countach is absolutely appropriate.

Above and top: Although the car itself didn't appear until late in 1988, the styling themes for the 25th Anniversary Countach were well under way by the late summer of 1987, smoothing the basic look back towards the first ideas, but keeping all the later aggression.

Below: The 1989 Anniversary model is in effect the last of the Countach line; the Countach philosophy will certainly continue in the next generation model, but the name itself will not be used again on the radically different new model.

PUTTING ON THE STYLE

Nuccio Bertone gave Lamborghini a styling house; Marcello Gandini gave him the Countach

IN THE HEADY WORLD of the supercar, there is one relationship which is important almost above all others, that between manufacturer and stylist. On that frequently tenuous link, the whole future of a project, even a company, can stand or fall.

When Ferruccio Lamborghini became a car manufacturer, he desperately needed a stylist to package the superb engineering wrought by his young team into a product the public could accept aesthetically – and which the style-conscious wealthy would be proud to buy.

He almost got it wrong at the start; his first 350GTV was shown in 1963 with a body by Carrozzeria Franco Scaglione, and the design was not at all well received. Lamborghini quickly switched the contract for the production car to a better-known house, Touring of Milan, and the next time the 350GT was seen it earned rave reviews. Such is style.

The relationship between Lamborghini and Touring might have been long and fruitful, but throughout 1964 and 1965 Touring's own financial problems worsened to the point where the company finally went out of business, and Lamborghini was effectively out in the cold once again.

LAMBORGHINI LOOKS TO BERTONE
Style and the man

It seems that, even at that time, Lamborghini knew the man he really wanted to style his cars was Bertone, but what followed was a stand-off of almost stage farce proportions, with neither side wishing to make the first move.

Nuccio Bertone is an obviously honourable man, and by the early 1960s the styling house that he still heads was one of the most famous in the world. The Bertone styling dynasty was founded in 1912 by Nuccio's father, Giovanni, who was born near Turin in 1884, into a farming family – much like Ferruccio Lamborghini's. At the age of twelve he went to work for a local firm as a true coachbuilder, building horse-drawn carriages. In 1907 he went to work for the Diatto car company, and around 1914 he started his own business building horse racing sulkies. Before long he began to build coachwork for cars, notably Fiat and Lancia, and although the company went through very hard times in the 1920s and 1930s it survived for his son to build into a considerable empire through the 1950s and expand up to the present day.

Nuccio was born in 1914, the year his father set up in business. He worked for the firm in his spare time but he also studied accountancy, which skill he took with him when he went to work for his father full time in 1932. With no formal artistic training it is fair to assume that his impeccable appreciation of style was simply inherent.

Nuccio divided his time through the 1940s and 1950s between going out into the world to sell the company's products, staving off the ever threatening financial crises, and going motor racing. From 1950 he managed the company, and in the mid-1950s he formed a link with wealthy American MG fanatic Stanley Arnolt, building Arnolt MGs and later Arnolt Bristols in such numbers as to make the company's future relatively secure. From the mid-1950s they went from strength to strength, building widely acclaimed show cars for Alfa, Abarth, Ferrari and anyone else who mattered, and expanding the coachbuilding side of the company.

In 1959 they moved to the big factory at Grugliasco in the suburbs of Turin, employing some 800 workers by the early 1960s, with an output of some 10,000 cars a year. They have never looked back, and that was the company in 1965 that Ferruccio Lamborghini knew he wanted to style his new cars.

BUILDING UP A RELATIONSHIP
Nuccio Bertone recalls

Nuccio Bertone talked about the relationship, in his spacious, stylish office at Grugliasco.

'Now, of course, we know that Ferruccio Lamborghini's personal wish was for us to design for him, but at that time I knew that he was working with Touring, and simply for reasons of fair play I didn't want to interfere with that relationship, so we never contacted Lamborghini.

'Lamborghini, for his part, felt that the reason we hadn't contacted him was not because of this fair play but because we didn't think of the Lamborghini as a reliable car!

'And so, in the few months before the 1965 Turin Show, Lamborghini sent about five different cars over to us. First of all, without announcement, a test driver brought a car to us and said that Lamborghini had told him simply to leave the car and the keys. Maybe a week later he would come back with another car and take the previous one away. That was how things began to happen; Ferruccio Lamborghini was sending these cars simply to prove that he wasn't sending just one specially prepared vehicle to impress us, but that these were his regular production cars!

'That was a way of working which has never happened to us before or since, but it had its effect. This man Lamborghini – who I still didn't know personally at the time – was maybe a rude man, but he was certainly frank and honest, sure of what he wanted and quite sure of the abilities of his car.

'And I was impressed with his cars. Through racing I had had a lot of contact with Ferraris and Maseratis and the like, but in the Lamborghinis there was the feeling of something completely different: in all of them, there was the perform-

Below: The Miura was a long way ahead of its time as a road car – mid-engined at a time when arch rival Ferrari was still sticking staunchly to tradition for his road cars. 'Eyebrows' around the flip-up headlamps are one of few styling tricks on the Miura.

ALFA ROMEO 33/2 CARABO
Forerunner of the Countach

The one car generally acknowledged as the real forerunner of the Countach was built by Carrozzeria Bertone in 1968, not for Lamborghini but as a styling prototype for Alfa Romeo. It was styled by Marcello Gandini and first appeared at the Paris Salon in 1968, as the Alfa Romeo 33/2 Carabo. Naturally enough, it was quite a sensation; rival stylist Sergio Pininfarina described the Carabo's lines and use of vivid colours as 'giving a pure, almost unreal beauty'.

The Carabo was based on Alfa's then current sports racing prototype, the Tipo 33/2. For racing, there had been several bodywork variations on the 33/2 (which had been introduced in 1967). There were two open versions (one of them dubbed the 'Periscopica', after its very high rear air intake scoop, the other labelled Mugello, after the racing circuit) and there was the aerodynamic 'Daytona' coupé, built by Alfa's Autodelta racing team in February 1968.

Like the racing models, and like the later Countach, the Carabo show car was of mid-engined configuration – in this case with a 90° V8 unit of just under 2 litres (122cu. in.) to suit racing regulations.

In the racers the power output had been quoted as 270bhp at 9600rpm but in the Carabo it was claimed to be 230bhp at 8800rpm, subliminally suggesting, perhaps, that the V8 had been detuned for the road, even though there was never any real intention of the Carabo being anything other than a one-off show car!

What was mainly interesting about the Carabo was its stunning, Gandini-styled bodywork. It was a real pioneer of the angular, lozenge shaped lines that would soon become so popular, but at a time when rounded aerodynamic shapes were still pretty much the in thing. Most distinctive of all was the unique door treatment which gave the car its name. Carabo is the Latinised version of Scarab, and the forward and upward hingeing doors and the vivid green

colouring were said to be suggestive of the wing cases of a beetle. They would carry over almost directly to the Countach, with their hydraulic strut counterbalancing and small, opening insets, which were partly for ventilation and partly to allow the driver just enough room to thrust out a fistful of lire to pay his *autostrada* tolls.

The Carabo used a new type of mouldable glass which allowed Gandini a lot more freedom with shapes than had previously been possible, and it used almost solely non-reflective materials in its interior, further pointers to later Countach solutions.

Finally, the Carabo also had to overcome the inherent cooling problems of the mid-engined layout, with rear-mounted radiators on this particular chassis, and it did it particularly neatly, with large scoops which simply followed the lines of the doors.

Below: The vivid Carabo – here under the close scrutiny of a younger Nuccio Bertone – was a real pioneer of the angular, lozenge shaped lines that would become popular later. Other Countach influences stand out quite clearly . . .

ance of course, but in the Lamborghini there was something more – it was a more pleasant car to drive on the road, a car more suited to customers.'

TOWARDS THE FINAL OBJECTIVE
Clothing the Miura

'All this happened before the 1965 Turin Show, where Lamborghini showed the chassis of the Miura – and *every* coachbuilder was interested in building something special on that chassis; which made Ferruccio Lamborghini even more surprised that I didn't go to speak to him too.

'And then one night I was walking through the halls with my wife after the show had closed and everything was quiet, and I took her to the stand to show her the Miura chassis. Surprisingly, Ferruccio Lamborghini was still there, and he stopped me and asked why I hadn't come along to ask him about the car just as everyone else had. He even asked me if I didn't *like* the chassis!

'I told him, of course, that I was very interested, but in a way I didn't want to ask him about it because of the Touring connection. I knew that Touring had done something on the chassis and I didn't want to interfere. In fact, Lamborghini did

not really like what Touring had done, but I had no way of knowing that.

'So that was the first contact, and even then I had the feeling that something very important was going to come from this in the future; I knew because I had my own strong wish to do something on the chassis, but I was also impressed by the strong personality of Ferruccio Lamborghini himself. There was a feeling even at that first meeting that something had worked between us . . .

'In this business, one of the most important things is to be able to go straight forward towards the final objective; I am always disturbed by long or frequent meetings; or by committees changing decision after decision. I prefer to have a counterpart who knows exactly what he wants, who is frank with me and who goes directly to the final objective. If we both have the same ideas, we can make them work.

'And Lamborghini had a lot of the right sort of people around him at the time: Dallara, Stanzani and so on, they were nice people and they were also superb engineers – but it was Ferruccio Lamborghini who was the successful one in

obtaining from them what he wanted and as quickly as he wanted it. He was very good at impressing on people the *spirit* of what he wanted; and, of course, if he hadn't got it from Dallara and the others he would have got it from someone else – he was so determined to get things done!

'He is a charismatic man who can influence other people and can get things done in half the time they all say is possible . . .'

THE NEW CHIEF DESIGNER
Exit Giugiaro, enter Gandini

Happily for Lamborghini, for Bertone, and perhaps for the whole future of the company – especially the Countach – all this coincided with the arrival at Bertone of the new chief stylist, Marcello Gandini. Incredibly, the magnificent Miura was the first car that Gandini ever styled, as Bertone confirmed.

'It was definitely the first car he designed; that happens all the time here with a new chief designer. When somebody comes here, I deliberately give them the responsibility of something big enough to show them that they can do things at least as well as their predecessor.

'In that year, Giugiaro had just left us and I wanted to have something on show in Geneva that would prove that, even though Giugiaro had left, Bertone were still in business and capable of doing great things – even better than before if possible.

'So we did three cars for that show: a Porsche 911 roadster, a Jaguar and the Miura.

'Gandini had never designed a car before; he was introduced to me by a supplier in 1964 and he had just done some interior designs, some furniture, a night club – but they all showed some special ability. I gave him a theme to show what he could do and when the results came back they were not very professional but there was something in the drawings that showed his ability to deal very well with the shapes of a car – and I immediately saw a talent in him that I knew could be built into professionalism . . .

'He had a very strange and difficult personality, and he found it very difficult to work as part of an organisation, or to work through meetings outside the company, but he was also very quick to learn from his mistakes and to listen to my side of things.'

FROM MIURA TO COUNTACH
Something completely different?
And eventually it was Gandini who styled the Countach, as Bertone explains.

'The Miura proved to be a very difficult car to drive, mainly because of its weight distribution; to drive it really well, you needed to be a racing driver, and many racing drivers who did drive it said that it was not the sort of car to be driven by just any customer.

'And so the first requirements for the Countach were to do not only something completely different, but also something that really could be driven easily on the road.

'That led to the idea of completely changing the engine alignment to improve weight distribution, but Lamborghini also set out to improve noise levels, comfort and even things like heating and ventilation. And as well as improving the engineering, from our side he wanted something at least as totally original as the Miura but with its own unique flavour.

Below: Paolo Stanzani, now the driving force at Bugatti, was brought in as a graduate engineer from the University of Bologna in the early 1960s, as Dallara's assistant. His unique back-to-front engine layout overcame many of the Miura's problems at a stroke.

Above: Ferruccio Lamborghini with Edoardo Miura, whose famous fighting bulls gave their name to the car. The bull theme was never far away from Ferruccio's projects; the wine he produces on his farm in Panicarola is called Bull's Blood.

'The doors, for instance, we had done this way on the Carabo, and it was quickly agreed that they were an acceptable solution for this type of "ultimate" sports car; and other things followed.

'With any other manufacturer, if we had displayed the first Countach we would never have *thought* of it as going into production, but with Ferruccio Lamborghini involved we were *sure* that it would be built – and not so much different from the way it first appeared . . .

'Our experience with the Miura was significant; in the beginning, at Geneva in 1966, I wasn't sure whether Lamborghini would dare to build that car exactly as we had done it, but by the end of the show he had so many cheques that he was able to go straight to production.

'With that experience, when the Countach was first shown, it was fairly clear that he intended to go straight in that direction again.

'Of course, there were some changes as the car developed. When we showed the first Countach, the lines were much cleaner, but as soon as we felt sure that Lamborghini was going to go into production we tried to do things the way they wanted them, although what we really *wanted* to do at the time was something much closer to the way the Anniversary car is now; that seemed the right approach even then.

'They did all the add-on things without asking us whether they were right or not – and at that time we had understood that they were only adding some of these things for testing purposes, for purely functional reasons. Only afterwards were we asked to do proper designs for the additions.'

PROBLEMS AT LAMBORGHINI
Dallara departs
'And then something more important happened: when the Countach project first started, I was sure we were going to have the chance to revise the design, because at that time we expected the car to be built in the Bertone works. But then things started to change at Lamborghini, because they began to have their own difficulties.

'When Dallara had been fired, I had a long meeting with Ferruccio Lamborghini at his home, trying to persuade him to change his mind and keep Dallara, but he wouldn't. In a fairly typical way he said that, alas, he didn't want him any more, that he could do without him and that there were other people capable of doing the job. Dallara was just one of them. That is an illustration of Lamborghini's character.

'And later, when they started having problems within the company, they decided (in fact, I advised them against my own interests) to build the Countach entirely themselves. We just agreed to send them our technicians and other specialists to show them how to start body production, how to set up the tooling and so on.

'This was at a time, before the Countach went into production, when we still had a regular commitment to Miura production, and there were already financial problems. Against that, Ferruccio Lamborghini could only plan to build the Countach at the rate of one car a week, and that was something which forced us to tell them that we preferred them to do their own production. So the chassis was manufactured with special criteria to have some parts of the body fitted, and we sent specialists again to help set up series production at Sant'Agata.'

It's an obvious question to ask, whether or not Nuccio Bertone found it easier to understand Ferruccio Lamborghini's problems, given the similar position his own company had been in in the early 1950s prior to the Arnolt era, but he was quite thoughtful about the answer.

'In a way the parallel is correct. We had the same sort of problems too in the early 1950s, which the Arnolt projects helped us to overcome, and that gave us the opportunity to expand the company, from (but still through) craftsmanship, to a higher level of industrial production.

'And in a way in those days Lamborghini were still in the first craftsmanship phase – of doing everything by hand. In the early days of the Countach, when they were only talking about one car a week, that was not really in our area anyway; it was simply too small a production, and

Above and top: The V8 Urraco was Lamborghini's attempt at breaking into the mid-sized market. It took its name from the fighting bull which killed the matador Manolete, and the Urraco almost killed Lamborghini too, failing to make any impact against the likes of Porsche and Ferrari and absorbing funds that the company could ill afford at a time when it was wracked with financial problems.

we had already grown a long way beyond that.

'As a good example, the Urraco was a model with which we tried to combine Lamborghini's technology with our in-house assembly to give a more modern system for manufacturing the car – and, of course, by building in bigger numbers we could have had a car that was much less exclusive than the Miura or the Countach. The plan for the Urraco was about 300 cars a year, and that *would* have worked with our sort of manufacturing set-up, where the Countach wouldn't.

'But if you put the Urraco in a showroom window, nobody would stop and look; if you put a Countach there, *everybody* would stop.'

Unfortunately, as the Countach arrived, Ferruccio Lamborghini was about to leave, and Nuccio Bertone felt that quite personally.

PADRONE NO MORE
A unique relationship ends

'When Lamborghini left, the whole relationship changed. Rossetti and Leimer, the new owners, were not cultured men in terms of cars in the way Lamborghini had been; they were just businessmen. They didn't buy the company because of the cars, they bought it looking for the maximum commercial return, and that was a very different approach.

'My relationship with Lamborghini was probably unique; we never actually had any formal agreement, and there were never any signatures; we just talked things out between us – to the extent that Ferruccio Lamborghini said, look, I'll do the engineering, you do the body, and we'll keep going.

'So, when you sell the company, the obligations are transferred too, but there *was* no formal agreement between us, and I'm not really the kind of man who could deal with the next management . . .

'Now, of course, the company is run again by professional people, and we have a relationship with Lamborghini once again . . .'

And, suddenly, it is clear how deeply personal the original relationship was between Lamborghini the car maker and Bertone the stylist.

'We keep in touch by telephone sometimes, but we don't meet very often. The last time was at the 25th Anniversary day. I still had the same sort of feeling. I was sitting at the table with Ferruccio Lamborghini and Lee Iacocca from Chrysler, and Lamborghini as usual was expressing his opinions very forcefully, but in a way that also said he was suffering because he was no longer the *grande padrone* of the marque.

'He felt a lot of regrets because the factory wasn't much changed from the way it was on the day he left, except that there was really no one there from the original team who created the name and the image. And he felt that although those who had followed had kept the name alive, nothing much else had really happened since then . . .'

Since the first Countach, in fact.

On the relationship, Bertone is clearly very emotional: 'It was, of course, a very, very special relationship – in many ways unique. In all my life I never experienced anything like it, and I doubt whether anything like it could ever have happened with anyone else, except maybe the very earliest days of the company when my father was dealing directly with Vicenzo Lancia.

'And when Lamborghini came to us it was a real challenge; Pininfarina had Ferrari – Bertone at that time was known for other cars, sports cars even, but not at all at the Ferrari level. With Lamborghini we gained a thoroughbred like the Ferraris. In economical terms it didn't mean anything, but for prestige it was everything.'

A CAR WITHOUT PEER
'Something extraordinary . . .'

And as for the Countach itself, Bertone has very few doubts.

'Cars like the Countach are not just GT cars or sports cars; they become a symbol of something more important, in which image becomes so high. For Lamborghini, the Countach has definitely meant the survival of the company, and for Bertone the Countach is important to this day; when you are talking with any other manufacturer about the possibilities for a new car, the Countach is always a point of reference, a way of understanding exactly what is needed, whether they want to be closer to or further from a car of that kind.

'I can't really say that it is a well or beautifully designed car – its beauty comes from something extraordinary, but it isn't a *classical* beauty. Sometimes there is a contrast between a clean design and the great *emotion* you feel from a car like the Countach, which is not a classically designed car but a car which through this strange and unique and exclusive shape gives you a suggestion of something extraordinary.

'Whatever else the Countach is, it is definitely a car that is a high spot in the whole history of sporting cars . . .'

* * *

When Marcello Gandini, the man who designed the Countach, went to Bertone as chief stylist in 1965, he was twenty-seven and he had never professionally styled a car. Yet within months of arriving at Bertone he had the glorious Miura to his name and was on his way to becoming one of the greatest stylists of all – and probably one of the least publicly known.

If you meet Gandini now, working alone from a marvellously tranquil studio in the grounds of his magnificent seventeenth-century villa in the hills outside Turin, you may partly understand why. He is withdrawn, almost shy, and he cares very little for the trappings of his art, only for the art itself. He doesn't own a supercar and he doesn't particularly want to, but it is very clear that he understands the genre.

EARLY DAYS, FIRST DESIGNS
Preparing for the Countach

He almost drifted into car design. His father was a classical musician and his family background was comfortably wealthy. Marcello started with an education in the Classics, but by the time he reached secondary school he was finding an interest in art. Alongside that he loved cars and he was always drawing sports cars and small racing cars, but at that stage he was more interested in the mechanical parts than in the styling.

He had no formal training as a designer, but taught himself. In 1959 he began to work, independently, as a designer, not with cars but on furniture, interiors, even a complete refurbishment for a Turin night club.

He first showed his work to Nuccio Bertone in 1963, through a friend, but with Giugiaro at Bertone as chief designer there was no place for a rival talent and it is no coincidence that Gandini did not join Bertone until Giugiaro left. He says now that he expected to stay for a few months; instead he stayed for fourteen years.

'My work there started with the Miura chassis shown at Turin in November 1965. At that time it was much quicker to work on cars than it is now; the project only lasted three months and the car was shown at Geneva in March 1966 – really as just a prototype, but it went into production.' It set the pattern for the Countach's arrival in 1971.

'Even the Countach was prepared in three months, because, again, it was really only supposed to be a prototype. There were really very few people working on these projects – maybe only two or three people in those days. And time was very short because you weren't working on a car that had to be ready to go on the road.

'Practically, the Countach was thought of originally as a prototype, but then with the experience of the Miura and knowing Lamborghini we always knew it was possible it would turn into a road car.'

PRODUCTION CAR CHANGES
Always improving

From 1971 prototype to 1974 first production Countach, there were quite a few changes, but far from feeling compromised by them, Gandini regards them very positively.

'From a styling point of view it wasn't so difficult to have to add the extra things onto the original. So far as the basic shape was concerned, very little was changed for the first road cars; the only big differences were the radiator ducts, and underneath to the materials and layout of the chassis. In the end, the changes really made the car better, because in the beginning it was very clean – in fact maybe almost too clean for a car. Afterwards, with the two big radiator scoops and so on, the car gained a lot more character – more feeling of power, and more aggression.

'It was the same later with the larger tyres; as the tyres and the wheels grew larger and the bodywork was extended to cover them, that also gave the car a more aggressive look. So changes

Above: Two of the greatest car designs of all time, the Miura (left) and the Countach; both were styled by Gandini. Although there were only five *years between the two, there is a world of difference in the philosophy; when Dallara designed the Miura, his mind was quite clearly on racing.* *Below: Gandini now works from his own studio, and nowadays the idea of styling a car like the Countach within a couple of months* *would be unthinkable. His designs for the Countach's successor were changed repeatedly by the new, American management.*

were made, but they always improved the look of the car. It was very good, for instance, to see what Wolf did with the car around the P7s. That was stimulating for the factory; if a customer decides to do something to the car that works, that is good in that maybe it prompts the factory to think about remodelling too.'

COUNTACH INFLUENCE?
Looking at the Lola T70

As for the basic influences on the Countach, it is obvious that the car was so spectacularly original at the time that there really were none, but in the past Gandini has said that if there was one car that inspired the Countach a little bit it was the

Above: Gandini will say that if there was any one car which helped to influence the overall proportions of the Countach, it was the Lola T70 sports car. The similarities are not in the lines especially, just in the proportions and in some of the T70's surfaces. The Countach, though, was never meant to be a racing car.

Lola T70 racing coupé. Now he will still broadly confirm that.

'The Countach was influenced to some extent by racing shapes – the T70 especially gave some lead to the overall proportions, just because I liked that shape. In fact, though, it is almost impossible to see the similarities because the cars are not really related at all; there's just a sensation of similarity. The only thing you can really say

that the Countach and the T70 share is their basic proportions first, and some surfaces. That was what was interesting on the T70, the treatment of surfaces, and that is where any similarity really is.

'The Countach never went into a wind tunnel because it just wasn't practical. There is a tunnel at the Turin Polytechnic but we could only use that with scale models – that was the only real testing we did and it was just to get a basic idea of the shapes.

'Remember, the Countach was ready in three months, so all we had was time to do the drawings and then immediately go into preparation of the car. If we had had, say, one year, the Countach would probably never have turned out the way it is

now because we would have had time to think more about the drawings and say – OK, well, this has to be changed. Since the Countach *was* so revolutionary it would undoubtedly have been different in the end had we had more time, more money, more people . . .

'Nowadays, you see, with the use of computers for instance, the only real difference is that some things are made easier, quicker – but a computer for a designer is really only another kind of pencil. The computer itself can't give you the ideas or any other ways of solving the styling problems. But the wind tunnel, on the other hand, will show up aerodynamic problems, and that's just one more problem to add to the progress of the car! As for the Countach, well, the car wasn't changed very much by using the tunnel. We did some minor things but the basic shape stayed the same'.

That the Countach is regarded as the greatest supercar of all has taken away none of Gandini's modesty, any more than the fact that the Diablo, after all the arguments, will also be his car. And it doesn't prompt him to own one.

'I've never been particularly interested in owning a Countach, or any of the other supercars I've designed; I've driven them but I don't want to own them. I'm much more interested in the cars of the future than ones from the past. As a designer you are enthusiastic when you first see the car, but when it is almost ready you are almost ashamed of it because you know there are things that you want to change even at the moment when it goes before the public.

'When a car is successful, when people like it, then I can get very fond of it too – that's a kind of nostalgia I suppose. It's a good feeling to see a Countach on the road for instance, because remembering the creation of it recalls not just the result but all the problems and all the people involved, and that's a good feeling.

'But drawing a supercar really is just like drawing a toy for collectors . . .'

S ANT'AGATA BOLOGNESE is a small town more or less midway between Modena and Bologna in the Emilia Romagna region of northern Italy. It is a small town like many another in this pleasant area of mixed agricultural and industrial Italy, but its name is known across the world wherever there are car enthusiasts, because on a smallish industrial estate situated on the outskirts of town you will find the Lamborghini factory.

SMALL BEGINNINGS
Home of a supercar

Sant'Agata isn't a big place by modern motor industry standards; it isn't even a big place by the standards of arch-rival Ferrari for instance, and its architecture is more or less anonymously early 1960s Modernism; its most distinctive external feature is the scalloped line of its roof parapet. That and the word 'Lamborghini' standing proud over the front façade.

It largely lacks the sometimes overbearing, stockade-like security of rival supercar makers like Ferrari and Porsche, and even from the small main road which passes the front gates you can generally see quite a lot of cars and activity.

What's more, once you have gained entry (because, appearances apart, you cannot simply walk in off the street) the Lamborghini factory has a remarkably cheerful, bright and informal feel about it.

It has expanded quite considerably since Ferruccio Lamborghini had it purpose built for his new supercar company in the early 1960s, but the feel has probably changed very little.

Behind the long front façade are the administrative and technical offices, on two floors, the upper floor looking out through gallery windows over the whole shop floor behind. To the left of that main building as you come in from the road are the customer services department, the development department and, upstairs, the staff canteens – where you are as likely to find president Novaro or chief engineer Marmiroli as you are to find the man who fits the windscreen wipers.

Below: *Standing out boldly in the flat Emilia landscape, the Sant'Agata factory, with its distinct scalloped façade, has seen its share of crises, but Lamborghini's future as a supercar maker finally* *looks secure under new Chrysler ownership. The factory is now due to be extended on to land behind, bought years ago, to make way for new models and increased production levels.*

BUILDING THE COUNTACH

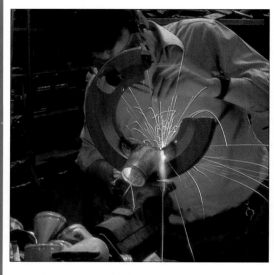

In a world where mass production rules, the Countach still relies on the human touch

Above: Final preparation of bodies before painting is hugely labour intensive, with every blemish rubbed out by hand until the surface is perfect enough to receive top coats of paint. Body coloured parts such as headlamp units and mirrors are prepared alongside main body shells for painting at the same time for colour match.

Below: Alloy and composite parts are assembled by hand on to Countach's light-weight superstructure, with all fitting and finishing done by hand and eye. Complex curvatures around NACA ducts in flanks and doors are among the most difficult parts of the shell to shape, and precise positioning of door lock plates is critical.

LAMBORGHINI PRODUCTION
Taking to the floor

The production area is in the main building, and, so far as Countach production is concerned, it is essentially split into five main areas. Chassis and body materials come into one end of the building, finished and raw mechanical components mainly come in the other. To the far right looking down from the gallery is the area where mechanical components are machined and finished. Directly below are the engine and gearbox assembly lines; these are not lines of conveyors as in a typical mass-production plant, but impeccably clean and orderly individual work stations at which the sequence of skilled operations takes place which eventually adds up to completed drivetrain units.

Beyond the machining section in the far right hand area are the paint and finishing shops. Dead ahead of the first floor gallery, behind the engine and gearbox lines, running directly down the centre of the main building towards the final test cells, is the final assembly line, based on individual work stations just like the rest of the operation. And even further back beyond that is the first leg of the essentially horseshoe-shaped assembly operation, where the chassis and bodies first come together on their slow journey towards the paint shop.

There are sub-assembly and trim making shops (and storage areas) in between all of this, of course; there are massive V12 marine engines interspersed with the Countach *quattrovalvole* engine lines; there are cars waiting for delivery; and on a separate line way over to the far side of the works, partitioned off from the Countach line, the massive LM off-roaders are taking shape. It is an impressive sight.

THE MANUFACTURING PROCESS
Clothing the chassis

The Countach manufacturing process really splits into three parts: body and chassis production, mechanical production, and final assembly. The body and chassis production takes bare chassis, and clothes them with alloy and composite panels to produce complete shells. The mechanical production side includes the machining and assembly of the drivetrain components (that is, engine and transmission) and chassis running gear (everything from suspension and brake assemblies to wiring looms, body parts and interior trim). The final assembly side comprises putting them all together into finished vehicles, painting them and testing them.

Body and chassis production runs effectively as a separate line from mechanical production. The complex multitubular spaceframes come to the factory complete and already painted from outside contractors Marchesi of Modena, a company with a very long and effective relationship with Lamborghini. Production of body panels (both metal and composite) is almost entirely done by hand. The metal panels (steel for the roof, rear bulkhead and inner doors, alloy of various thicknesses – but mostly extremely thin – for the majority of the shell) are bent and beaten here. And the composite panels (glassfibre for the inner chassis tub and wheelarch eyes, for instance, and more exotic

Above: Endless care is taken with hand fitting of every Countach door frame. No two doors are exactly alike and fitting can take

many hours. Even then, all door furniture has to be added and finished units are one of the last things to be added to each Countach.

Below: The whole process begins at one end of the factory as the bare multi-tubular chassis and its lighter superstructure pass

along the line to the jigs where basic body panels are welded, rivetted or bonded on. Chassis in foreground already has floor in place.

carbon fibre and Kevlar units for the new sills and spoilers) are moulded and cured here.

As the chassis moves along the line on its own individual trolley, the panels are rivetted, lapped and welded into place, initially on very large jigs, later with the finishing touch of hand and eye. Most of it, although obviously extraordinarily skilled, is relatively straightforward, but fitting the unique, forward and upward hingeing doors is recognisably the most complex part of the whole operation. Like everything else, it is done entirely by hand, and there are never more than a couple of craftsmen working on any one operation at any one work station.

Essentially, each Countach door is given its final contours by hand (beating the soft, alloy outer skin with a bewildering assortment of esoteric tools) and its alignment is endlessly refined until it fits precisely the aperture in the body shell to which it will eventually be permanently married. The fitting operation is complicated by the need to continue the lines of the NACA air ducting vent from door to body shell, and to accommodate the subtle curvature of the side windows. It is patently more art than science . . .

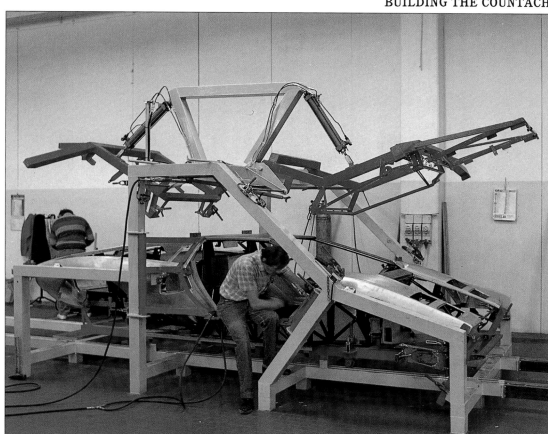

Right: This complex jig at the very first stage of body fitting ensures that the panels are accurately aligned, but the actual fitting is done largely by hand, with seams and flanges being hammered on to formers to give strength to the growing structure.

THE PAINT SHOP
More than skin deep

When, eventually, the shells are complete (including the GRP mouldings which line the floor, much of the inside of the engine bay, and the front compartment – plus the outer composite panels) they pass through to the paint department. Here, they are brought (largely by hand rubbing and smoothing) to the level of finish which will eventually accept the paintwork, the philosophy being that if what is underneath the paint isn't right, the paint finish itself never will be. Also within this department, separate but body-coloured outer components such as headlamp covers and a multitude of trim parts are prepared, and these go into the spray booths on the same jig as the main shell to ensure final colour matching.

Lamborghini, unlike large scale manufacturers, and even larger supercar manufacturers like Ferrari, do not have automated final painting procedures; the shape of the Countach is so complex in places that it simply would not be feasible on this scale. Instead, each car is individually hand sprayed in dustproof spray booths which have flowing water beneath the floors and constant clean air circulation (and each car is individually hand smoothed between each of its numerous base and finish coats).

However brilliant the finish at this stage, this is far from each Countach's final visit to the finishing department, as any blemishes picked up on the assembly lines or during final road testing come straight back here for rectification.

Above: Each Countach body shell goes into the paint spray booth with all moveable panels such as doors, engine cover, boot lid and so on mounted on a single jig, for spraying all at the same time from the same paint batch. A perfect colour match is guaranteed.

Below: Final painting is done by hand in spacious booths with constant air circulation and running water below the slatted floors to keep airborne dust in check. Cars eventually undergo minute inspections of paintwork and any faults are rectified before line.

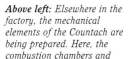 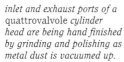 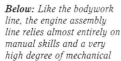

Above left: Elsewhere in the factory, the mechanical elements of the Countach are being prepared. Here, the combustion chambers and inlet and exhaust ports of a quattrovalvole cylinder head are being hand finished by grinding and polishing as metal dust is vacuumed up.

Below: Like the bodywork line, the engine assembly line relies almost entirely on manual skills and a very high degree of mechanical sympathy. Cylinder heads and their camshafts are now being fitted, with every nut or bolt torqued down to a precise value.

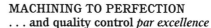

Above right: With an engine nearing completion, the ignition distributor is here being fitted to the end of one cylinder head, from where it is driven from the end of one camshaft. This is a carburettor engine, but fuel injection is also used for some markets, notably the US.

MACHINING TO PERFECTION
. . . and quality control *par excellence*

Elsewhere, while the chassis and bodies are being prepared to this pre-assembly stage, the mechanical components are being machined and fabricated in their own areas of the factory. Again unlike, say, Ferrari or Porsche, Lamborghini do not have their own foundry or forge, and basic engine and transmission castings and forgings come in from outside suppliers, to be finished here on a mixture of machines from basic workshop lathes and grinders to ultra-sophisticated computer controlled multi-operational machine tools.

In the middle of the whole machine shop is a toolmakers area, setting and maintaining the machine tools to their critical tolerances and specifications. And next to that, shielded from the rest of the factory by glass walls but pointedly visible to everyone, is a quality control office which uses state-of-the-art technology constantly to monitor both quality of materials and standards of production.

From this machining area of the factory, the basic building blocks of engine and transmission emerge: cylinder blocks, the complex sump with its integral transmission transfer tunnel, the four-valve cylinder heads, camshafts, crankshafts, gears, casings and covers.

Everything, notwithstanding the precision of the machine on which it has been produced, is finally checked by eye and finished by hand. It all exudes more of the feeling of a large racing workshop or a huge, high-quality restoration operation than of a contemporary car manufacturer.

ASSEMBLY LINES
Working by touch, by eye

From here, the parts go to the bright, spacious mechanical assembly lines directly below the gallery windows – the gearboxes to one line, the engines to another. Each unit is built with ultimate care and attention to detail; you will see endless examples of engineers working by touch and by eye, constantly cleaning and lubricating every moving part, checking fits, refining detail.

And when the basic engines are built, the bought-in components like electrical equipment, ignition systems and fuel systems (carburettors

Below: The massive V12 engine and transmission unit are fitted into the car as a single assembly, around halfway along the line of work stations. This particular engine is a US spec fuel-injected unit, in contrast to the carburettor engine on previous page, which is for less emission-sensitive European markets – with the advantage of slightly more power.

for European cars, injection for the USA) are gradually added from the endless racks of waiting parts, until the completed engines are lined up in ranks to await their chassis.

In between, every engine and every gearbox is carefully bedded in, by being run first by electric motors and then under their own power in the test bays, a long and expensive process but one which ensures that every unit is ready for the road test which eventually follows, and ultimately ready for the customer.

Finally, the two distinct lines, body and drivetrain, come together to begin the process which produces the finished cars.

The painted chassis/body units (still mounted on their individual trollies, but without the precious doors fitted) start their journey along the final line by having the plumbing, major control cables, air-conditioning systems, wiring and rear lights fitted.

By this point, each Countach already has its final identity affixed, in the form of its chassis plate number – and there will be a separate sheaf of paperwork to specify any individual requirements on each and every car.

FINISHING TOUCHES
Emerging from the cocoon

As it passes along the line, the shell is fitted with its steering column, pedal assembly, its basic front and rear suspension assemblies and the water radiators. Further along comes more wiring, the interior sound insulation, the hydraulic systems, the rest of the suspension parts, the brakes and the driveshafts.

About halfway along the line of work stations, the engine and transmission are carefully guided in from an overhead hoist as a single major unit, and its exhaust system is also threaded into the steadily filling engine bay at this point.

Above: Stages of final assembly, as wiring and plumbing are fitted, engine and suspension are added and car edges towards trim assembly stages. Each car has a specific identity long before this stage, **centre right**, and precisely what goes in here is defined by specifications on sheet. At **bottom left**, foreground car shows engine cover fitted. Engine now neatly, and massively, in place.

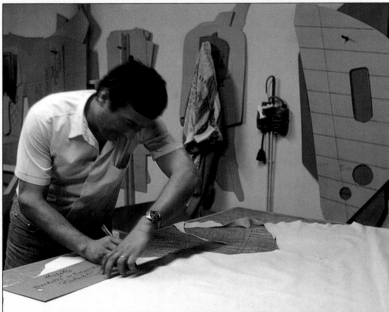

Above: From below the line, a good view of one rear suspension corner and the outboard end of the driveshaft passing between the twin coil spring and damper units. The flat, ribbed component is the engine sump, including the final drive, and the massive brake calipers can be seen inside the wheel. Every suspension joint has racing type adjustable bushes for accurate setting of geometry.

Above: Interior trim parts such as seats, **top**, and dashboard, **above**, are almost entirely finished by hand, mostly using selected leather from vast stock of hides, **centre**. The trim shop occupies its own area of factory, close to the final assembly line, and the customer can order almost any combination of colours and materials. Trim is also fitted on the line, directly into the body shell.

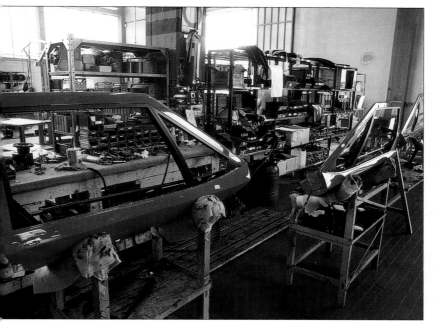

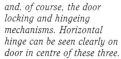

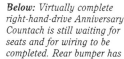

Above: Getting closer to completion, the doors await final furniture items like window lifts, glass, electric mirrors and their controls

and, of course, the door locking and hingeing mechanisms. Horizontal hinge can be seen clearly on door in centre of these three.

Below: Virtually complete right-hand-drive Anniversary Countach is still waiting for seats and for wiring to be completed. Rear bumper has

also to be fitted – now to same spec on all models and much neater than older 'federal' type, which did nothing for the car's looks.

Above: Even at this very late stage in production process, with doors fitted and car obviously nearing completion, there are still a

thousand small things to be done. Once each car is complete, it will be checked in minute detail and then both bench and road tested.

With the main mechanical components now largely complete, the creature comforts start to go in, with interior trim, the door locks, carpets and glass. The front wheels are on by now and the separate bumpers on US spec models, plus headlights and the big wiper motor. Fitting the windscreen is another major operation, involving a great deal of time-consuming hand-fitting of the trim around the aperture, and then some nerve-racking placing and bonding.

The dash moulding is in now, and more carpeting and more trim, already covering most of the wiring and plumbing and making the car begin, suddenly, to look relatively neat and complete. The door seals are fitted, though not the doors themselves; they are still away in a separate area being fitted with glass and mirrors and motors and trim and the like, amid endless pampering.

The car looks even more finished as the rear wheels go on and the gearlever knob is fitted, although there are still no instruments in the yawning holes of the dash. The steering wheel at this stage remains where it has been, for some unaccountable reason, ever since the car came onto the line – on the roof.

Finally, the last of the trim goes into the boot, the door kick plates are fitted and, at last, the doors themselves slot impeccably into place.

When it is finished, every Countach is minutely inspected, road tested, adjusted, tested again and only when absolutely everything is right does it finally pass out of the factory – past the large notice that has been there from the time the factory opened: *'Il prossimo collaudatore è il cliente; fate in modo che resti soddisfatto'* – 'The next test driver is the customer; make sure that he is satisfied'.

At the end of it all, you can slide down to within inches of the ground, insinuate yourself over the broad sill into the steeply reclined seat behind the chunky steering wheel and ponder that all the design talent, all the engineering and craftsmanship in this building, all the 1000 or so manhours of assembly and love that go into each individual Countach, finally comes down to creating a little ultra-quick world a few feet square and a bare three feet high for two incredibly lucky people to savour at their leisure.

THE COUNTACH DISSECTED

A unique blend of unsurpassed style, near racing car technology, and unashamed luxury

MECHANICALLY, THE COUNTACH is everything a supercar should be. By late 1980s standards it isn't technically sophisticated in the new-generation electronic sense, but some of its engineering solutions remain unique. It isn't the fastest car in the world any more (if it ever was), but what challengers there are, without exception, have to qualify their claims behind the mask of 'limited editions'. It *is* still the most uncompromising of all its genre; and it will always have an indefinable aura that nothing else, be it Ferrari GTO or F40, Aston Zagato, or Porsche 959, has yet managed to capture. Tell an outsider that the Countach *isn't* the fastest car in the world and chances are he simply won't believe you.

Essentially, the Countach is a car like any other, with obvious elements such as chassis, engine, transmission, suspension, brakes, bodywork and so on, that between them take in every significant feature.

It is in those obvious elements' frequent departures from the commonplace that the Countach becomes great.

MAKING OF A SUPERCAR
Something more than adequacy
Any road car relies on a combination of factors to achieve its purpose. In an everyday car that might include practicality, luggage space, economy – adequacy. In a car like the Countach, adequacy isn't enough. A supercar has to combine the power for ultimate performance with the chassis' ability to handle that power, and it has to allow the driver to be not just peripheral, but an important, thinking part of the package.

It is almost automatic when talking about high performance cars to talk first about horsepower and capacity and torque and the number of cylinders, but without a place to mount it the best engine in the world is no more than a design exercise. The same follows for the most sophisticated suspension, or the best brakes or the prettiest body: without a chassis to hang them on they are all useless.

THE CHASSIS
A platform for excellence
The chassis is the platform for everything else to be built into or to hang from. In itself it has to perform a number of functions: it has to be strong enough to accept all the mechanical loads; it has to be rigid enough in both bending and twisting modes to provide a rigid platform from which the suspension can work effectively; it has to have the structural integrity to withstand impacts if ever it is asked to, while protecting the occupants from injury; it has to provide acceptable space for those occupants and their occasional luggage, and it has to do it all without weight penalty for the engineer, cost penalty for the manufacturer, or aesthetic penalty for the stylist.

It is not an easy task.

Mass production cars nowadays achieve all those objectives cheaply and repetitively in vast numbers with a unitary construction shell, in which the body *is* the chassis, relying for its strength on the egg-shell-like monocoque principle. The tooling needed is too complex and therefore too expensive to be feasible for small production numbers, but it does extend as far up the scale as the Porsche 911, for example.

On the other hand, cars like the Testarossa and the Countach use a separate chassis with the unstressed body mounted onto it. Both Testarossa and Countach use spaceframe chassis (in which there is more space than frame). In the case of the

COUNTACH CUTAWAY

Above: The Countach shows its unique engine and transmission layout, with the gearbox effectively between the driver and passenger, the complex spaceframe, and the twin coilspring and damper units of the rear suspension. The car shown here is a fuel-injected quattrovalvole to US spec, which before the Anniversary model meant it *was sullied with the ugly add-on bumper pads front and rear. The fuel tanks can be seen low down between the doors and the rear wheels, the radiators high up on the shoulders under the big air scoops, and the exhaust silencers behind the final drive unit and under the rear luggage compartment. The large rear wing was, of course, strictly optional.*

Testarossa it is made from a relatively small number of quite large tubes; in the Countach it is made from a very large number of mainly small steel tubes.

To achieve the strength it requires, the Countach chassis relies on classic spaceframe geometry, in which each individual tube, so far as is practically possible, feeds only either compression or tension loads (not bending loads) into the other tubes which it joins. In effect, the whole chassis comprises a series of linked, triangulated units which work together to give a unit of enormous strength but very little weight.

In the Countach chassis, the main elements form two massive side sills, a large central tunnel, two extremely large rear side structures to support the engine and rear suspension, a box-like front structure to pick up the front suspension, and the panelled cross-linking elements which form the bulkheads. On top of this main load-bearing chassis there is also a lighter tubular superstructure which simply supports the upper bodywork. Seen naked as it arrives at the factory, it looks both immensely complex and immensely strong – and it is both.

SUSPENSION
Constant development, unchanging principles
The suspension which it supports has changed a great deal in detail over the years to refine the Countach's handling, roadholding and ride, the biggest changes coming with the adoption of the new generation super-low-profile tyres in 1978 on the 400 S.

SPACEFRAME

Left: The Countach's chassis is an immensely strong tubular spaceframe. It has massive side sills and a large central backbone, as well as a lighter superstructure which supports the shell.

In fact the Countach was originally intended to use a new design of Pirelli low-profile tyre which Lamborghini were helping to test in the early 1970s. That tyre never went into production, however, so the original Countachs used the then current state-of-the-art low profile Michelins until the change to the even wider Pirelli P7s, which were apparently quite similar to the tyres originally being evaluated.

Tyres notwithstanding, the Countach's basic suspension layout hasn't changed at all in principle. Like any suspension system, its joint objectives are to give the occupants an acceptably comfortable ride on all types of road surface, to protect the structure of the vehicle from damaging shock loads, and to keep the tyres (the chassis' one and only link with the road surface) firmly in contact with the ground.

Most mass production cars are allowed to compromise ultimate roadholding for comfort, and to forego ultimate sophistication for cost saving. Once again, a supercar like the Countach has to make few compromises.

Its wheelbase is reasonably short, at 98.4in. (2500mm). That's a couple of inches shorter than the Testarossa, for example, but fully 9in.

(228mm) longer than the compact Porsche 911. The front track is wide, at 60.4in. (1536mm) and the rear is even wider, at 63.2in. (1606mm).

CLASSIC GEOMETRY
Wishbones all round

At the front, the Countach uses unequal length double wishbones, with coil springs and telescopic dampers, plus an anti-roll bar to control body roll. At the rear it has a similar system, but in place of the upper wishbone is a lateral link and a trailing arm, and for the bottom link there is a reversed wishbone and trailing arm. This is still effectively a double wishbone system, but wider based and feeding the additional loads from the driven wheels forwards into the chassis to give the necessary 'anti-squat' geometry under hard acceleration. There is a substantial anti-roll bar at the rear too, again to control body roll, and where the front has a single coaxial coil-spring and telescopic damper unit, the rear has two coil-spring/damper units on each wheel, with the short driveshafts from the final drive unit passing between them.

All the suspension links are made up in racing fashion from very high strength tubular material,

and every joint on the Countach's suspension uses sealed-for-life racing type metallic ball joints with plastic inserts – not so harsh as the all-metal bushes of a pure racing set-up, but not so unacceptably flexible as the rubber bushing of a typical production car.

Every major joint is adjustable, for fine-tuning the suspension geometry on each individual chassis. That means the toe-in, castor and camber of each wheel can be adjusted independently to give exactly the designed parameters.

This suspension carries the massive cast hub-carriers which in turn support the brakes and the alloy wheels.

BRAKES
Power to tame the Countach

Braking on the Countach is by very large disc brakes all-round, with racing-type four-piston calipers on each wheel. The front discs (which, although working on a smaller tyre footprint, do most of the work, as weight transfers forward during heavy braking) are 11.8in. (300mm) diameter and the rears are 11.2in. (284mm) diameter. There is vacuum servo-assistance (for more power without unacceptably high pedal pressures) and there are two independent hydraulic systems for safety, but there is no anti-lock system. The handbrake works mechanically, on the rear discs, and the lever is low down between the driver's seat and the big central transmission tunnel.

In the final, 25th Anniversary Countach, the whole lot sits on a new pattern of composite light-

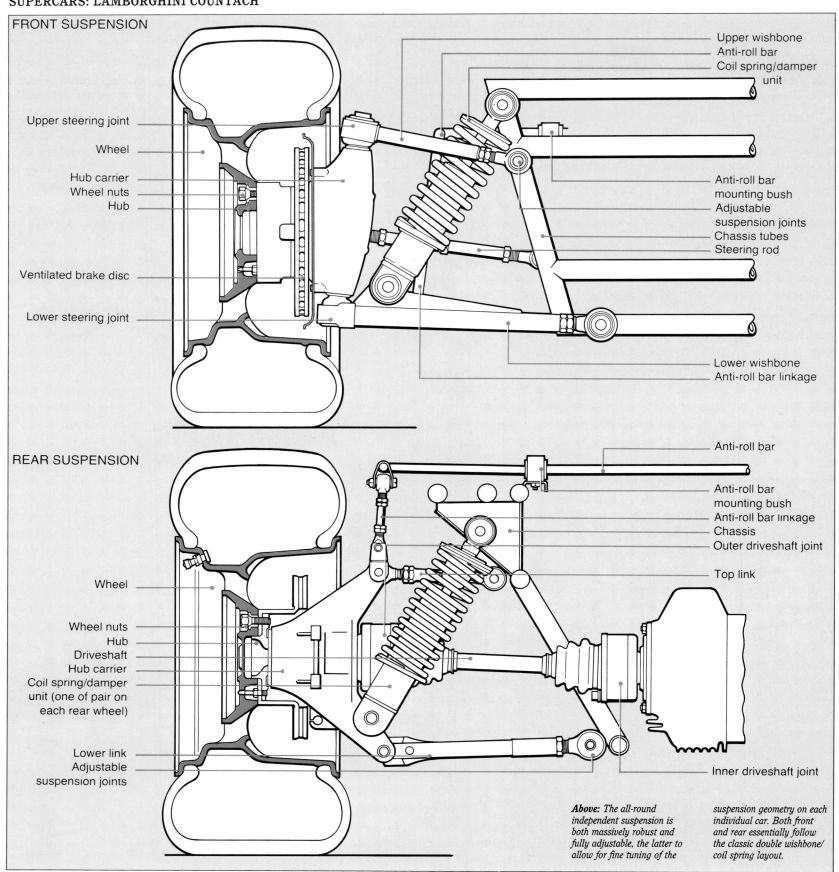

FRONT SUSPENSION

Upper steering joint

Wheel

Hub carrier
Wheel nuts
Hub

Ventilated brake disc

Lower steering joint

Upper wishbone
Anti-roll bar
Coil spring/damper
unit

Anti-roll bar
mounting bush
Adjustable
suspension joints
Chassis tubes
Steering rod

Lower wishbone
Anti-roll bar linkage

REAR SUSPENSION

Wheel

Wheel nuts
Hub
Driveshaft
Hub carrier
Coil spring/damper
unit (one of pair on
each rear wheel)

Lower link
Adjustable
suspension joints

Anti-roll bar

Anti-roll bar
mounting bush
Anti-roll bar linkage
Chassis
Outer driveshaft joint

Top link

Inner driveshaft joint

Above: *The all-round independent suspension is both massively robust and fully adjustable, the latter to allow for fine tuning of the suspension geometry on each individual car. Both front and rear essentially follow the classic double wishbone/ coil spring layout.*

alloy OZ wheels (held by five bolts) and Pirelli P Zero tubeless radial tyres.

These latest wheels have a cast alloy centre which bolts into a forged alloy rim, which is stronger than a simple cast type. At the front, the wheels are 8½JJ×15in. and the tyres are 225/50ZR15s, running at between 37psi and 40psi (2.6–2.8bar). At the rear, the wheels are 12JJ×15in. and the tyres are 345/35ZR15s, with pressures between 40psi and 43psi (2.8–3.0bar) depending on driving speeds. The higher pressures are specified for speeds of over 160mph (260kph).

The spare wheel (which lives under the front hatch, along with the battery, the brake and clutch

hydraulic systems, the steering rack and the windscreen washer system) is a narrow, space-saver type, with a 105R 18X Michelin tyre. It is purely a 'get-you-home' device with a maximum speed limit of 62mph (100kph).

On this latest version of the car, although the wheel and tyre sizes are the same as they were on the previously P7-shod cars, the tyres are quite different; on this next new generation of Pirelli tyres the tread is asymmetrical as well as being unidirectional. On the P7s the tread was the same pattern across its width; on the P Zero both the tread pattern and the compound change across the width – hard and almost devoid of tread on the

outside, softer and with more water drainage channels on the inside edges. The idea is that the harder you try the more you get the car to work on the 'dry' area, while still retaining enough water-clearing capacity for wet roads.

The driver's link with the Countach's sophisticated suspension system and those fat Pirelli tyres is an unassisted rack and pinion steering layout with a collapsible steering column to meet legislation worldwide, and just over three turns of the small, leather-bound steering wheel from lock to lock.

Lamborghini quote the Countach's turning circle as 42.6ft (13m), which, given the strictly limited visibility from the cockpit and the negligible front-end ground clearance, does demand a certain amount of care when turning in restricted spaces, especially given an overall width of 78.7in. (2000mm).

BODYWORK
Steadily changing face

One factor in the Countach's favour though is that its overall length, at 165.4in. (4200mm), is really quite compact. The Testarossa, for instance, is over 11in. (285mm) longer and even the seemingly very chunky 911 with its much shorter wheelbase is almost 10in. (250mm) longer. The Countach is actually shorter too (by an inch) than the supposedly compact Ferrari 328 GTB, almost exactly the same length as the front-engined Porsche 944, and very close to Ford's booted Escort, the Orion saloon!

Maybe it says something for the Countach's aggressive looks and proportions that so little car has so much presence. The outward appearance is one thing which has changed fairly regularly, but the Countach's visual impact never has.

Where the car *has* changed principally is in the areas of cooling ducts, wheelarches, bumpers and aerodynamics.

The big changes in the first of those came very early in the Countach's life, even before it went into production, when the large, boxy air scoops were added on the shoulders behind the doors and the NACA ducts were incorporated into the flanks.

Both those modifications to Gandini's clean original shape were to help solve the prototype Countach's serious overheating problems.

COOLING SYSTEM
Resisting compromise

Those problems were partly due to the large V12 engine's natural tendency to run hot, but more to the Countach's unconventional approach of putting the radiators in the rear of the car instead of in the nose where they would have the benefit of natural airflow, albeit at the expense of a compromised nose shape.

The Countach resisted the compromise and the production cooling system still uses radiators mounted at the rearward flanks of the car, high up behind the doors under the big scoops. Air passes into the cooling system through the boxes and the NACA ducts, through the big square radiators (helped by dual fans on each) and out via the louvres on top of the rear wings. The smaller air-ducting strakes in the sill extensions that first appeared on the 1988 car are functional too, but for cooling the rear brakes rather than the engine cooling system.

The system has been modified again on the Anniversary car, both externally and internally. Externally, the ducts are now slightly better integrated into the overall shape, and internally, the radiators have been repositioned, with a single large fan to each, instead of the two smaller units, and the engine has been given higher capacity water pumps.

The wheelarches changed very substantially, of course, when the Countach gained its wide-tyred look, and on the latest model the arches are even more neatly integrated – part of the overall look

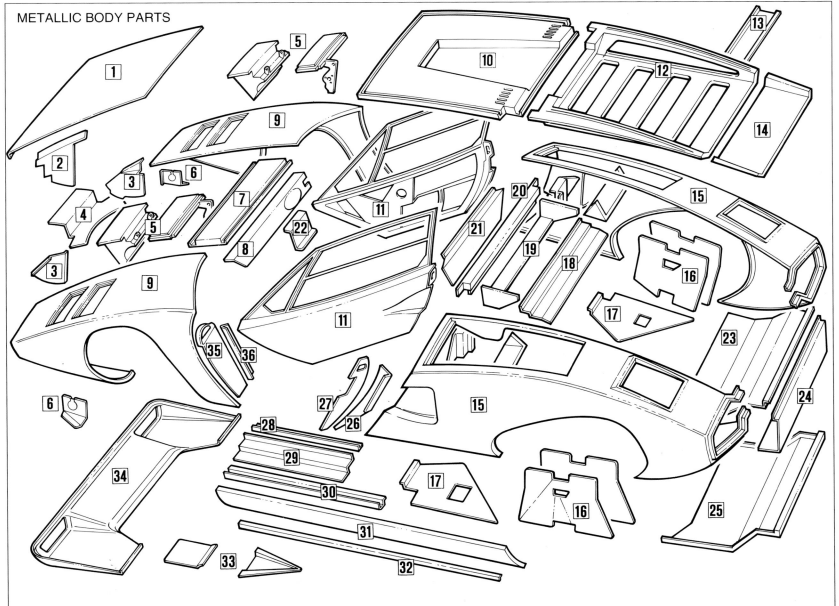

METALLIC BODY PARTS

1 Bonnet panel	8 Bulkhead	16 Petrol tank	24 Number plate	29 Sill covering	
2 Bulkhead	9 Wheel boxes (front)	17 Petrol tank guards	cross-bar	30 Piping container	
3 Bulkhead condensers	10 Engine cover	18 Water duct	25 Lower rear	31 Mounting	
4 Support	11 Doors (unclad)	19 Cross-bar	lining	32 Foot rest	
5 Headlights	12 Engine cover lining	20 Cross-bar cover	26 Door striking	33 Rear air intakes	
6 Bulkhead torsion bars	13 Bulkhead	21 Bulkhead	plate	34 Lining	
7 Lower windscreen	14 Boot cover lining	22 Support	27 Cover, door lock	35 Door cover	
panel	15 Wheel boxes (rear)	23 Boot panel	28 Lower door sill	36 Spacer	

Above: The Countach uses a combination of alloy, steel and composite panels. This diagram shows the individual alloy panels, mainly hand-formed, which are assembled onto the light upper superstructure to form the majority of the shell. The steel roof is not shown.

which in a sense takes the final Countach some way back towards the plain look of the first.

One of the bigger changes that happened at the prototype stage was an aerodynamic one, prompted by the fact that the first car had too *much* aerodynamic downforce on the front end.

One of the problems that Stanzani's longitudinal engine layout had been designed to overcome was the Miura's unfortunate nose-lightness, which could even result in the front end lifting aerodynamically at near maximum speeds. In fact the Countach's weight distribution, at 42/58 per cent front to rear, is very little different from the Miura's 45/55, but the superior aerodynamic downforce of the short, wedge-shaped nose makes a substantial difference overall. On Gandini's original prototype, the nose was even more steeply raked and the front lid was slightly recessed. In this guise, the first prototype has so much front downforce that the rear end could become worryingly light under very heavy braking from high speeds, and so by the time the last of the three prototypes appeared, the slope had been reduced by raising the bumper level slightly and the luggage lid was no longer recessed.

AERODYNAMICS
Wings and things

Some aerodynamic changes have been rather less subtle than that, and the most obvious one is the large, optional rear wing. It certainly gives the Countach an even more aggressive stance, but most of the test drivers will tell you privately that that is all it does – except to sap a noticeable amount from the top speed through its inevitable drag effect. In reality, the basic shape of the Countach is so aerodynamically stable and the front-to-rear balance now so good that the wing is certainly not an essential.

The rest of the external changes over the years have been largely a matter of tidying and refinement, with the biggest changes coming on the

*Below: A considerable amount of tidying up was done with Anniversary model's styling, **right**, notably from the boxy airscoops of earlier cars,* *left, and around the rear bumper area to make the car, at last, acceptable with one rear bumper design for both the American and European markets.*

1988 model with its sill strakes – and, of course, on the 25th Anniversary car.

On this final Countach, the engine cover is different too, and so are the air exit louvres on the rear upper wings, while even more of these body components now rely on the use of composite materials, which has increased steadily through successive models.

The 25th Anniversary car now uses composite panels for the wheelarch 'eyebrows' and the lower sill extensions, for the new rear bumper, for the engine cooling ducts, for the whole engine cover, for the front compartment cover, the luggage space cover and the front air-dam.

Above: New style composite wheels with Pirelli P Zero asymmetric tyres are one of Anniversary Countach's most distinctive visual changes. Lamborghini still haven't worked out an acceptable way of incorporating 'universal' bumpers on nose of car. This example is the neat European spec.

The majority of the body, of course, is still panelled in very thin, hand-formed aluminium sheet, attached to the chassis and its lighter tubular superstructure. The body doesn't bear any of the chassis loads and in fact in many places it is so thin that it can be bent simply by leaning too hard against it – such is the quest for supercar lightness! The floor of the car and the interior of

the engine bay are made from glassfibre but the general construction method is still very much alloy-bodied and hand-crafted, although the roof, the rear bulkhead panelling and the inner door panels are of steel for additional strength.

The most distinctive feature (and the most pampered during the production process), the vertically hingeing doors, are actually quite simple in principle. They hinge at the top end of their forward edge, just below the window line, and they are counterbalanced by small hydraulic struts which can be seen between the front door edge and the door frame. The door windows do not open as such but they have a small panel set into them which does wind down (initially with a manual winder, now electrically) for a degree of ventilation, but mainly for paying *autostrada* tolls, for instance, without having to leave the car.

There is no apparent mention in the driver's handbook of the supposed 'grenade-pin' system for freeing the doors if the car happens to be inverted . . .

The headlamps are raised automatically by electric motors when needed and the only real luggage storage space is in the rear compartment (with its own separate cover) behind the engine bay. According to Lamborghini it has a capacity of 7.5cu.ft (240 litres), in practice it will take little more than a couple of conveniently-shaped cases, so it is best to travel light.

Finally, one aesthetic area in which the Anniversary Countach has made a great leap forward is in the bumpers, which have always presented problems on Countachs for the legislation-sensitive US market. Now, the rear bumper is 'universal' and very neatly integrated, but in the past, US cars have been forced to wear some really quite hideous add-on units. (see the cutaway of the US-specification Countach on pages 34 and 35). Even the latest car still has to have an additional front bar for the USA, but at least it isn't so nasty as in the past.

Above: This car has the straked sill additions as introduced late in 1987, plus a body-coloured front bumper and US style rear panel. It doesn't have the rear 'bumperette' pads, which were an ugly but unavoidable answer to US legislation at the time.

Below: The distinctive vertical door opening style of the Countach is more than a styling gimmick: it is a very practical way of allowing occupants into and out of an already wide car where clearance is limited. A clever counterbalance system uses hydraulic struts.

DOOR MECHANISM

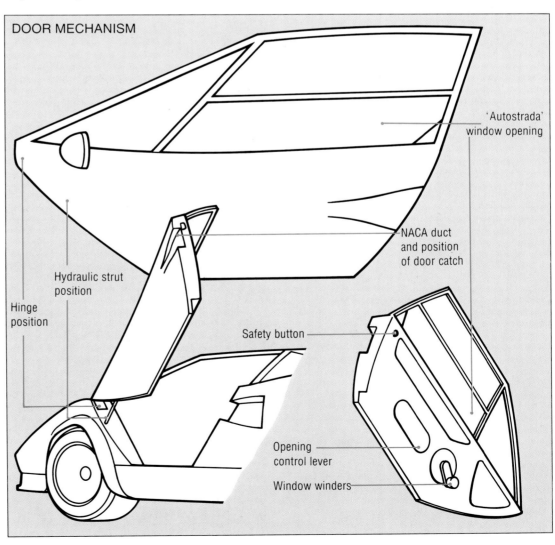

'Autostrada' window opening

NACA duct and position of door catch

Hydraulic strut position

Hinge position

Safety button

Opening control lever

Window winders

THE ENGINE
Continuing a classic line

And so to the mechanical elements beneath the skin that go to make the Countach what it is – and that really means, of course, the glorious V12 engine and its unique drivetrain.

One thing that's worth remembering about the Countach engine is that although it has undergone a fantastic number of successful changes over the years, even the current generation 5.2-litre (317.3cu.in.) four-valve per cylinder *quattrovalvole* engine can trace its line directly back to the original 3.5-litre (213.5cu.in.) two-valve Lamborghini V12 from 1963. And with Lamborghini starting from a clean sheet of paper at that stage, the engine that in effect has seen Lamborghini through their whole history to date had no previous Lamborghini tradition, no in-house experience, and above all no parts bins to draw on. It was designed from scratch.

The man who Ferruccio Lamborghini employed to create that first V12 was yet another inspired choice, in the same way that Dallara and Stanzani had been on the engineering side, and Wallace was for the development role.

GIOTTO BIZZARRINI
An engine in months

The man Ferruccio employed was former Ferrari engineer Giotto Bizzarrini, and, although he was slightly older than the others, he was still only in his mid-thirties when he went to Sant'Agata.

His background was absolutely classical motor engineering. He was born near Florence in 1926, his father was himself a mechanical engineer and a prosperous landowner. Giotto gained his degree in mechanical engineering from the University of Pisa in July 1953, and by that stage he was already firmly hooked on the automobile side. For his university thesis he had designed and built an air-cooled 750cc four-cylinder twin-cam engine for the ubiquitous Fiat Topolino – and like any young, car mad Italian of the time, he had carried out all sorts of other modifications on the little Fiats.

For a time after he graduated, he worked at the university as a lecturer, but in 1954 he went to work for Alfa Romeo, as a chassis test engineer in their experimental department. He stayed with Alfa until February 1957 when he made the jump every engineer dreamed about, to Ferrari.

His time there was enormously successful, not just as an engine designer, but also as a chassis engineer and aerodynamicist. Above all else, he will remain famous as the man who designed and developed the legendary Ferrari GTO, which won the world sports car manufacturers' championships in 1962, 1963 and 1964.

By that time, though, Bizzarrini had already left Ferrari, in the famous mass walkout of November 1961 when Ferrari lost most of his top engineers over rows about policy. Several of them, including Bizzarrini, became involved with the interesting but short-lived ATS sports car project, and as that foundered, Bizzarrini, as a freelance designer, did several designs for Renzo Rivolta's US V8-engined Iso and Rivolta cars.

He left Rivolta in 1963, just as Ferruccio Lamborghini was head hunting for the best engineers in the business, and there was no doubt at all that Bizzarrini was one of them. What particularly interested Lamborghini at the time was the knowledge that Bizzarrini had designs under way for a four-cam V12 1½ litre Grand Prix racing engine, for the formula then current. Lamborghini saw in that small racing engine the basics for the 3.5-litre (213.5cu.in.) V12 which he planned for

his putative Ferrari-beating road cars.

Like everything else in the Lamborghini story at this time, the engine was commissioned, planned, designed and built with almost frightening speed, so quickly in fact that at least one respected British motoring historian, LJK Setright, has suggested that the engine was really designed under a secret contract by Honda.

That theory doesn't seem to find any credence

elsewhere, but the one irrefutable fact is that the first Lamborghini V12 went from drawing board to test bench within four months, running for the first time in mid-May 1963. And it seems that it was rather more than Ferruccio Lamborghini had bargained for.

He had certainly planned to outgun Ferrari with his new V12, both in terms of power and refinement. He was aiming for 350bhp, not from the

obvious expedient of simply making a bigger capacity unit, but by more sophisticated design, notably in using four cams instead of the two which were then normal on Ferrari's V12s. His engine, at 3.5 litres (213.5cu.in), would be smaller than Ferrari's biggest unit of that period, the 4-litre (244cu.in.) Superamerica, but bigger than his Maranello rival's much more widely used 3-litre (183cu.in.) 250 series, and, it is true to say,

considerably more modern than either of them.

With 350bhp it would beat both the 400's 340bhp (though not the very rare early version's claimed 400bhp) and the 280bhp of the most potent 250s. Bizzarrini had a personal interest in extracting as much power as possible from the engine too, as he was due to be paid on a sliding scale against horsepower – more for beating the planned 350, less for missing it!

Above: Bosch fuel injection and associated de-toxing equipment on latest Countach quattrovalvole *engine does sacrifice a small* amount of power but at least makes the car saleable in emission sensitive markets. Engine and ancillaries are a squeeze in big engine bay.

In the event, he met the target quite handsomely, at least in terms of output, with an official quote of 360bhp at 8000rpm and perhaps as much as 370bhp 'off the record'.

Above: Almost complete engines on the mechanical assembly line show narrow angle of vee, compact layout of twin camshafts on each cylinder head and tight run of exhaust manifolds. Tunnel through sump for final drive transfer shaft is below the light flywheels.

Below: A huge array of machine tools in factory, **top right**, is a tiny part of inventory of equipment needed to machine crankshafts, **bottom left**, from solid billet, and to machine and assemble components for Countach five-speed manual gearboxes, **bottom right**.

Right: Neat simplicity of a finished Countach interior belies the complexity of systems that are buried under the trim. Most of wiring and plumbing goes into car at a very early stage, as here, and is subsequently covered by dash, inner sills and carpets.

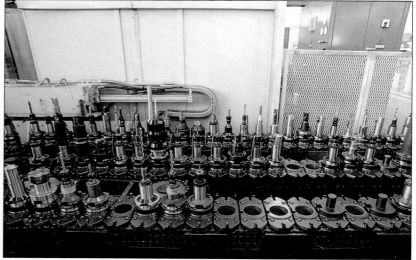

REFINEMENT v POWER
What Ferruccio wanted

But while Ferruccio Lamborghini may have been delighted with the numbers, he hated most other things about the engine. He had been looking for roadgoing refinement and had got what he saw as not much more than a raw racing unit. Bizzarrini, disillusioned because he realised Lamborghini had absolutely no intentions of letting him start a racing programme, left Sant'Agata virtually as soon as the engine was running and Dallara was given the job of smoothing off the rough edges and turning it into something which could be used in a road car.

When he had finished with it it had lost its racing type dry-sump lubrication system, gained sidedraught rather than downdraught carburettors (cheaper, and easier to fit under a sleek front-engined car's bonnet) and the power had dropped to a still respectable but very much more civilised

270bhp at 6500rpm, with torque dropping less dramatically, from 240lb ft at 6000rpm to 239lb ft at 4000.

That is essentially the engine which gradually evolved into today's Countach units, and it is worthwhile just recapping on the basic types which have appeared in successive Countachs.

The story goes that the original prototype had the 5-litre (305.2cu.in) engine which gave it its LP500 designation, and according to Bob Wallace it did, but only very, very briefly. The engine had been tested quite extensively on the factory dynamometer, but apparently when it was put into the car it expired within the hour, blowing up in a big way at high speed on the *autostrada* during its first outing with Wallace at the wheel. It was never rebuilt and all subsequent testing was done with the 4-litre unit with which the car was eventually launched for production in 1973.

That was the 3.23 × 2.44in. (82.0 × 62.0mm)

3929cc (240cu.in.) engine with four overhead cams, two valves per cylinder and six twin-choke sidedraught Weber 45DCOE carburettors. It gave a claimed 375bhp at 8000rpm on a compression ratio of 10.5:1, and peak torque of 266lb ft at 5000rpm.

That had evolved by 1978 into the milder but more manageable 353bhp/267lb ft engine of the LP400 S – without changing any major dimensions but with many internal modifications to improve driveability for the average customer.

Less power, for whatever reason, was hardly the point of the Countach, of course, and the first step towards rectifying the balance came in 1982 with the 3.37 × 2.7in. (85.5 × 69.0mm) 4754cc (290cu.in.) unit for the LP500 – with 375bhp at 7000rpm and 302lb ft of torque at 4500rpm.

The biggest change of all came in 1985, with the introduction of the four-valve-per-cylinder *qv* cylinder heads and a final increase in capacity.

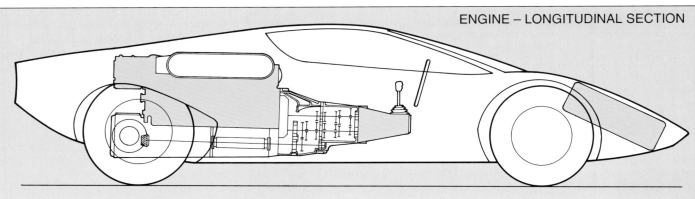

ENGINE – LONGITUDINAL SECTION

Right: The unique layout of engine, gearbox and final drive which allowed Stanzani to package the Countach so compactly. Engine (shaded) drives forward to five-speed gearbox with change at extreme front end and with minimal linkage. Drive then goes via simple drop gear set and back via short driveshaft through sump, to final drive unit at rear.

ENGINE – CUTAWAY

THE ENGINE TODAY
Four-valve sophistication

This still current Countach engine has its twelve cylinders set in a 60° vee. The bore and stroke of 3.37 × 2.95in. (85.5 × 75.0mm) gives a capacity of 5167cc (315.2cu.in.) and the internal architecture is still very much as it has always been, but refined to a very high degree.

The crankshaft runs in seven main bearings and each bearing cap is held down with four bolts for strength. The connecting rods are of forged steel and the pistons are of forged light alloy.

The four overhead camshafts are driven by chains and operate four inclined valves per cylinder – two inlets and two exhausts – set around a single central spark plug in a pent-roofed combustion chamber. The inlets now enter in the centre of the vee (whereas they originally went in between the two camshafts on each head) but still point almost directly downwards for exceptionally free gas flow (four small valves give better flow than two large ones for the same amount of valve lift, with less strain on the valve gear); the exhaust ports are on the outside of the heads, feeding into tubular steel manifolds and then to a transverse dual silencer system behind the final drive.

On European specification Countachs the fuel system (fed from twin tanks in the chassis just behind the doors and below the radiators) uses two electrical fuel pumps and six twin-choke downdraught Weber 44DCNF carburettors; for the

Above: Heart of the matter – this cutaway of a fuel injected version of the quattrovalvole engine, plus gearbox and final drive, shows the four valves per cylinder and the clever layout. Gearbox, to right in the picture, points to front of car, final drive is at back.

Below: Latest Countach heating and ventilation system offers push-button control of temperature and hot and cold air circulation from central panel, behind gear lever. Temperature is shown digitally on panel and six large vents along top of dash keep the screen clear.

AIRFLOW

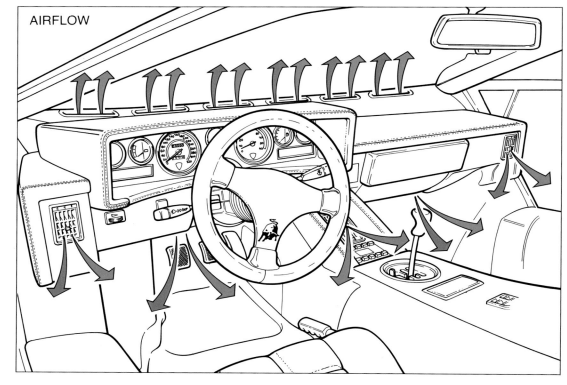

Below: Countach cockpit is strictly two-seater, but there's nothing particularly claustrophobic about it, thanks to huge glass area and extensive use of light trim. Big side sills provide a platform for sliding in, and with the deep central tunnel they also provide very firm sideways location once you are settled in.

more emission-conscious US market the de-toxed engine is fuel-injected, using a Bosch K-Jetronic system. The fuel fillers are set into the rear part of the NACA ducts, behind the door releases.

The engine's electronic ignition system (with a single distributor driven from the 'rear' of the engine) is all by Marelli and incorporates a rev limiter.

With what the current handbook says is an 8.0:1 compression ratio (Lamborghini originally quoted 9.5:1), today's European version gives a quoted output of 455bhp at 7000rpm and a maximum of 369lb ft of torque at 5200rpm. The injected and de-toxed US version sacrifices very little in either power or flexibility and still gives a very adequate 425bhp.

THE TRANSMISSION
Effective and unique

With the gearbox and final drive unit, this forms the heart of the Countach. In Stanzani's uniquely effective layout, the power is taken forward from the end of the crankshaft through a hydraulically actuated, self-adjusting single dry-plate clutch, forward to the five-speed manual gearbox between the driver and passenger, with the short, vertical gearlever acting virtually directly into the 'box.

The gearbox ratios are all indirect, at 2.232, 1.625, 1.085, 0.858, and 0.707:1, with a 1.960:1 reverse. From the gearbox output, the power is taken through a simple set of drop gears to the shaft running back through the sump (in a sealed tube) back to the final drive unit on the rear of the engine block.

The final drive has a clutch-type limited slip differential and a ratio of 4.09:1 and from there the drive goes to the rear wheels through short, universally jointed driveshafts running between the twin spring/damper units on each side.

The layout has the advantage of pushing the main mass as far forward in the car as possible for better weight distribution, but without intruding into the passenger cell as much as a 'conventional' mid-engined layout with the engine ahead of the gearbox. It is slightly heavier overall, and it does raise the centre of gravity slightly by forcing the crankshaft to run above the power transfer, but not by as much as the contemporaneous Ferrari Boxer, whose flat-12 motor was actually located above its gearbox, with the crankshaft above the axle line.

INSIDE THE COUNTACH
More function than luxury

All this can propel just two people and their luggage at speeds close to three miles per minute, in a cockpit that couldn't really be called luxurious, but which is undeniably functional – with a clear and comprehensive seven-dial instrument layout, a steering wheel adjustable for both height and reach, and something close to the feel of a sports racing car in its layout and proportions.

In its latest versions, the Countach has even finally made some previously frowned on concessions to creature comfort. The two seats are now electrically adjustable for reach, height and back rake (via three switches in the door-sill oddment compartments), the 'toll' windows are electrically operated, there is central locking and even air conditioning, Lamborghini having finally accepted the slight power loss implied by the engine-driven refrigeration pump.

In the overall scheme of the Countach, the 'softening' changes were minor, and the basic character of the car has changed very little since it first took the motoring world by storm in the early 1970s. It is still one of the most individual cars in production, still right up there with the world's greatest supercars. Whether the Chrysler regime will let that character continue unchanged into the next generation 'Countach' remains to be seen . . .

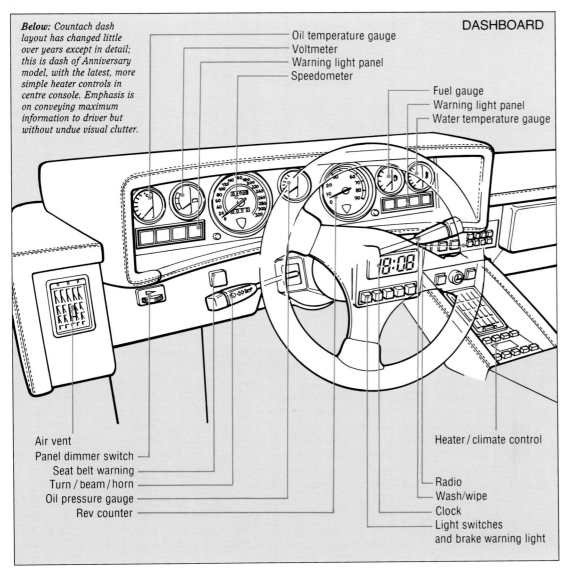

DASHBOARD

Below: Countach dash layout has changed little over years except in detail; this is dash of Anniversary model, with the latest, more simple heater controls in centre console. Emphasis is on conveying maximum information to driver but without undue visual clutter.

- Oil temperature gauge
- Voltmeter
- Warning light panel
- Speedometer
- Fuel gauge
- Warning light panel
- Water temperature gauge

- Air vent
- Panel dimmer switch
- Seat belt warning
- Turn / beam / horn
- Oil pressure gauge
- Rev counter

- Heater / climate control
- Radio
- Wash/wipe
- Clock
- Light switches and brake warning light

DIMENSIONS

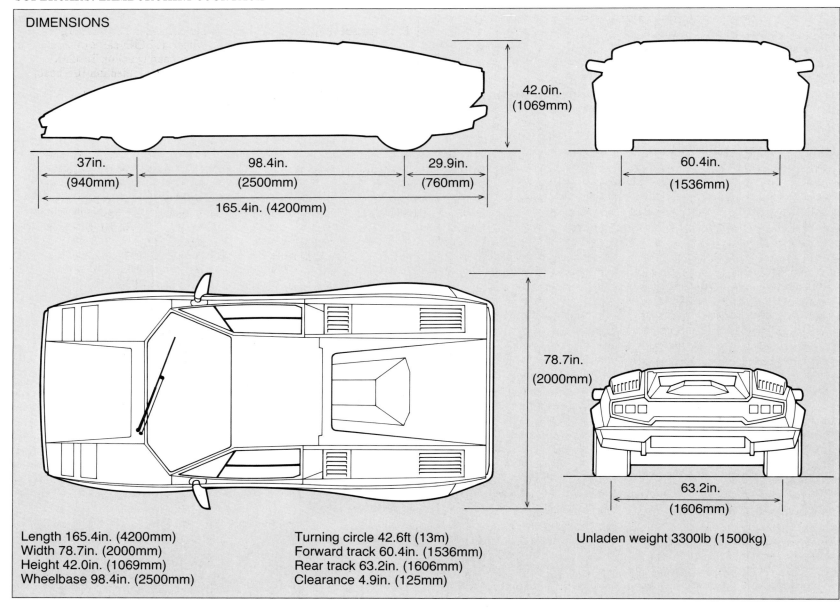

37in. (940mm)   98.4in. (2500mm)   29.9in. (760mm)

165.4in. (4200mm)

42.0in. (1069mm)

60.4in. (1536mm)

78.7in. (2000mm)

63.2in. (1606mm)

Length 165.4in. (4200mm)
Width 78.7in. (2000mm)
Height 42.0in. (1069mm)
Wheelbase 98.4in. (2500mm)

Turning circle 42.6ft (13m)
Forward track 60.4in. (1536mm)
Rear track 63.2in. (1606mm)
Clearance 4.9in. (125mm)

Unladen weight 3300lb (1500kg)

Below: *A familiar sight after all these years on the roads around Sant'Agata, but the locals still stop in their tracks as the Countach goes by.*

Right: *Over the years, the Countach's power output, shown by pink bands, has managed to stay ahead of main rivals Ferrari, even if it* *has sometimes been quite a close run thing. Today, Countach power is beaten by Porsche 959 and Ferrari F40 – both limited editions.*

COMPARATIVE POWER OUTPUTS
(European spec where appropriate)

MAXIMUM POWER OUTPUTS – LAMBORGHINI v FERRARI

1971	COUNTACH LP500 (Prot.)	440bhp @ 7400rpm
	365GTB4 DAYTONA	352bhp @ 7500rpm
1973	COUNTACH LP400	375bhp @ 8000rpm
	365GT4 BB BOXER	344bhp @ 7000rpm
1977	BB512 BOXER	340bhp @ 6200rpm
1978	COUNTACH LP400S	353bhp @ 8000rpm
1982	COUNTACH LP500	375bhp @ 7000rpm
	BB512i BOXER	340bhp @ 6000rpm
1985	COUNTACH 5000qv	455bhp @ 7000rpm
	TESTAROSSA	390bhp @ 6300rpm
	Limited Edition 288GTO	400bhp @ 7000rpm
1986	Limited Edition PORSCHE 959	450bhp @ 6500rpm
1988	Limited Edition F40	478bhp @ 7000rpm

bhp 0   50   100   150   200   250   300   350   400   450

LAMBORGHINI COUNTACH 1989 'ANNIVERSARY' MODEL
Specifications

Engine	Engine type	60° V12; naturally-aspirated; water-cooled; four overhead camshafts; longitudinally mid-mounted
	Displacement	5167cc (315.2cu. in.)
	Bore	3.37 in.(85.5mm)
	Stroke	2.95in.(75.0mm)
	Compression ratio	8.0:1
	Max. quoted power (DIN)	455bhp @ 7000rpm (425bhp in US spec, with fuel injection and catalyst system)
	Max. quoted torque (DIN)	369lb ft @ 5200rpm (340lb ft @ 5000rpm in US spec)
	BHP per litre	88.0 (82.2 in US spec)
	Power/weight ratio	308.8bhp/ton (288bhp/ton in US spec) (unladen weight)
	Fuel tank capacity	26.4 Imp. gal. (31.7 USgal./ 120 litres)
	Cylinders	Light alloy block with iron cylinder liners; steel crankshaft with seven main bearings; wet sump lubrication
	Cylinder heads	Light alloy; twin chain-driven overhead camshafts on each cylinder bank, operating four valves per cylinder
Fuel system	Type	Six twin-choke downdraught Weber 44DCNF carburettors (European spec) or Bosch K-Jetronic fuel injection (US spec)
Electrics	Ignition system	Marelli AEC 104 BK-780 electronic ignition, with rev limiter; Marelli distributor and coil
Transmission	Gearbox	Five-speed manual, located in front of engine with drive being returned to rear-mounted final drive unit via transfer shaft running in sealed tube within engine sump
	Gear ratios	Top 0.707
		4th 0.858
		3rd 1.085
		2nd 1.625
		1st 2.232
		Reverse 1.960
	Final drive ratio	4.091:1
	Clutch	Single dry plate; hydraulic operation
Suspension	Front	Independent, by unequal length double wishbones, coil springs, telescopic dampers, anti-roll bar
	Rear	Independent, by upper lateral link and radius arm, lower reversed wishbone and radius arm, dual coil spring/telescopic damper units on each side, anti-roll bar
Brakes	System	Ventilated discs all round, 11.8in.(300mm) diameter front, 11.2in.(284mm) diameter rear; four-piston calipers; dual hydraulic circuits; vacuum servo-assistance; mechanical handbrake operating on rear discs
Steering	Type	Rack and pinion, 3.15 turns lock to lock
	Turning circle	42.6ft(13m)
Wheels/tyres	Type	Composite light alloy OZ wheels, 8½JJ×15in. front, 12JJ×15in. rear; Pirelli P Zero tubeless radial tyres with asymmetric, unidirectional tread, 225/50ZR15 front, 345/35ZR15 rear; Michelin 105R 18X 'spacesaver' spare
Structure	Chassis	Multitubular steel spaceframe with light tubular superstructure, steel rear bulkhead
	Bodywork	Mainly unstressed alloy panels, except for steel roof, steel inner doors, steel bulkheads; glassfibre floor and engine bay lining; composite wheelarch finishers, lower sills, rear bumper, engine cooling ducts, engine cover, front compartment cover, luggage compartment cover, front bumper and air dam
General	Unladen weight	Approx 3300lb(1500kg)
	Overall length	165.4in.(4200mm)
	Wheelbase	98.4in.(2500mm)

DRIVING THE COUNTACH

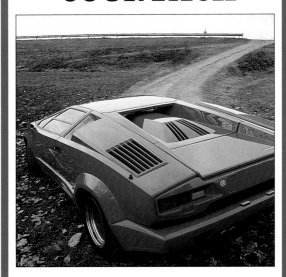

Even in the ranks of the supercars, the Countach is a car set apart by performance and poise

EVEN FOR THOSE FEW PEOPLE who are fortunate enough, on a regular basis, to drive and analyse what we all cheerfully call 'supercars', the thrill rarely wears off. However many Porsches, or Ferraris, or Aston Martins, or Lamborghinis you drive, you will always be back for more; supercars are definitely addictive.

Like any other car, their performance, their handling and roadholding characteristics, their practicality such as it is, are necessarily comparative. But in the end what you feel about any supercar more often than not adds up to something much less objective than simple numbers, much less rational than everyday practicality, and certainly nothing so tedious as considerations of price. They have character, but they also have entirely different characters, and different supercars suit different sorts of people.

A dyed-in-the-wool Porsche 911 buyer, for instance, would never buy a 928 – they may as well be different marques as different models; and a Ferrari buyer would never go near an Aston Martin, whatever its capabilities.

COUNTACH
The supercar testers' choice

The supercar as a genre *is* a supercar largely because it transcends all those perfectly logical criteria which any thinking buyer will apply to a real world saloon or hatchback. The supercar exists on a heady mixture of massive performance, staggering roadholding abilities, head turning looks and sheer charisma. The only value for money aspect that anyone is likely to be remotely concerned about is selfish entertainment value.

Most writers who are lucky enough to write about supercars regularly are not burdened with the problem of which one to buy, and in that respect at least can approach the subject with something of the same detachment as the super-wealthy real-life buyer who can take his or her pick. For the title of ultimate supercar, most go straight for the Countach.

They go by heart and not necessarily by head – straight for those outrageous, provocative looks; they go for the promise of more power than any other car on the road, for the thought that if no one has conclusively proved that a Countach *will* do 190mph in two directions on a straight and level road, no one has conclusively proved that it won't either; and they go for the unrivalled indi-

viduality of the Countach even in this sort of exclusive company.

FIRST ACQUAINTANCE
Getting to know the Countach
Even blindfolded, you would recognise a Countach the moment you go to climb into it, from those still unique, vertically hingeing doors. To open them you press a button in the upper edge of the door section of the NACA duct and lift. The doors are big and heavy (especially so on the latest model with its electric window lifts) but the hydraulic counterbalancing struts do their job perfectly (so long as you're on a level surface – slopes can confuse the balance) and the doors lift easily. That leaves a decent sized opening through which to climb into the car, but it *is* rather near the ground;

the Countach stands just 42in. (1069mm) tall from road to roofline.

Your next problem is the enormously wide, padded sill which covers the side pontoons of the complex spaceframe chassis, but this comes in useful as an intermediate platform on which to park your bottom prior to sliding down into the leather covered seats and, on the driver's side, insinuating your legs under the low, chunky steering wheel.

Pull down the door, helping its counterbalanced

Below: Even without the big rear wing, and with the neater tail treatment of the latest bodywork, rearward visibility is not the Countach's best feature! The view is essentially limited to the top of the engine cover through the no more than letterbox-sized rear window, and of radiator air scoops in both door mirrors.

weight down with a firm final shove to ensure the catch is properly closed, and you are in.

From here on, the Countach becomes far more conventional, although with more of the feel of a luxuriously trimmed racing car, perhaps, than of a mere road car.

INTERIOR
Confined but comfortable

The cabin is actually quite wide, but so much of its width is taken up by those sills and the big central transmission tunnel that the seats themselves are deeply sandwiched in the two remaining gaps. In fact, at around 18in. (460mm) wide, they have perfectly adequate hip room, and the generously padded, beautifully trimmed sills and tunnel provide reassuring lateral location without feeling intrusive.

There isn't a great deal of headroom, however, especially for anyone of six feet or over, and the dramatic inward curve of the side windows towards the narrow roof can leave your head noticeably close to the angle of roof and door.

That said, it isn't at all uncomfortable or claustrophobic, especially as Lamborghini are sensible enough to use very light trim for most of the interior.

Until the 25th Anniversary model came along, the Countach's seats were of the genuine one-piece bucket type, with the angle between squab and back fixed. They adjusted for reach and they rocked slightly to give a degree of inter-related adjustment of rake and height, but it was not over-generous and the driving position tended to be rather knees-up and laid back. The latest car has more conventional seats, which look less sporty but offer a lot more adjustment. Now the back will rake separately from the squab and there is adjustment for height as well as reach – and all of it controlled electrically, from three neat buttons in the small, lidded cubby holes in the side sills.

Aside from those tiny cubby holes, there's not a great deal of room in the cockpit for oddments – just small pockets in the doors (deeply recessed to keep the contents in when you open them) and a smallish, lidded glovebox in front of the passenger. It's just about possible to slot a book of maps (or anything similarly flat) behind the seats, providing you don't have them all the way back, but that's just about it.

On the other hand, there is a reasonable space (preferably for soft cases) in the tail, with its own separate cover behind the engine cover, both opened from pull levers in the door jamb. The front lid opens from a pull button below the dashboard but there is little room for more than a crumpled up jacket in that compartment, as it is already pretty well filled with frame tubes, the spacesaver spare, the steering rack and the brake and clutch reservoirs.

SETTLING IN
Control familiarisation

In arriving at a comfortable driving position you also have the advantage of being able to adjust the steering column for both rake and reach, via a single lever below it. Some of the advantage of that is lost, though, by the still slightly knees-up stance and the fact that the footwells are necessarily narrow to fit in between the side chassis

Left: Forward visibility is a lot less problematical, with the huge, steeply sloping screen looking out over a nose which is so short and stubby that is almost *disappears from view from the driver's seat. Corners are quite easy to judge, but ground clearance is almost non-existent, so take care near high kerbs.*

members, and they are angled quite markedly inwards.

The pedals are angled in too, but they are big enough and well spaced, except that there is virtually nowhere to rest your left foot to the side of the clutch. The handbrake emerges from a slot on the central tunnel, very low down by the driver's seat, and the shortish gearlever rises vertically from a six-fingered gate on top of the tunnel, just a hand's turn from the thick leather steering wheel rim.

The Countach's minor controls are all very conventional, in fact almost disappointingly parts-bin looking. There are two steering column stalks: the left one controls the lights, turn indicators and the horn, the right one controls the windscreen washers and the big, single pantograph wiper. The switchgear has moved around to some extent over the years, but on the latest car the push/push switches for the brake check, rear fog lights, hazard warning lights, dipped beam and parking lights are in a row down to the right of the steering column.

There is a digital clock just above them and space for a radio in the centre, and there is a large interior driving mirror in the centre of the screen, which gives you a very good view of the engine cover but not much else.

CLIMATE CONTROL
Considerably improved

To the left of the steering column is a dimmer-switch for the instrument panel lights and on the centre tunnel console, ahead of the gearlever, are two switches for the central door locking (now standard), a cigarette lighter, and the pushbuttons and digital temperature telltale for the much improved climate control system. There are also separate door lock controls on the rear corners of the doors themselves, and the driver's door has a fingertip control for the electrical exterior mirror adjustment.

Behind the gearlever are an ashtray and the switches for the electric window lifts, but it is still only those tiny vents that open.

As for other ventilation, the Countach has vents all along the top leading edge of the dash for clearing that huge screen, at the ends and the centre of the dash for warm or cold 'face-level' ventilation, and deep in the footwells for thawing or cooling the feet.

INSTRUMENTS
Everything you need to know

Finally, the Countach has a full complement of instruments, set quite high in front of the driver over the steering column in a large, single, rectangular binnacle, deeply recessed to cut down as much as possible on stray reflections, and generally quite well placed for easy visibility.

Graphically, though, they are not the Countach's best feature for the driver. The faces are black and the lettering mainly white but the design tends to fussiness rather than the stark clarity of, say, a Porsche. The information is there all right, but so are a lot of extraneous graphics and visually over-heavy black rims.

The main instruments are a large matching speedometer and rev counter, flanking the steering column. The former reads to 320kph (equivalent to 199mph!) in 20kph increments; the latter

reads to 9000rpm, by thousands, with an orange sector starting from 7000rpm and a red sector from 7500rpm to 500rpm beyond the V12's power peak and backed by that electronic rev limiter to protect the frighteningly expensive engine from accidental damage.

The other instruments are smaller and set symmetrically around the speedo and rev counter. To the left are an oil temperature gauge and a voltmeter; to the right are the fuel level gauge and the water temperature gauge. Right in the centre, between the two big dials, is an oil pressure gauge, the layout showing that Lamborghini expect the Countach driver to give the mechanical priorities of engine revs and oil pressure the respect that they deserve.

If the driver is negligent about less important matters, however, there are warning lights below the left-hand instruments for headlamps, parking lights, hazard lights and handbrake; below the right-hand instruments there are reminders for turn indicators, rear fog lights and low battery charge; and down to the left of the steering column is a warning to fasten your seat belt. The last of those should hardly be necessary if starting the Countach's mighty V12 isn't warning enough in itself that you should be firmly belted in.

STARTING PROCEDURE
Time for a little care
That starting demands a little bit of attention to technique, at least on European-specification, carburettored cars. First you switch on, with the key in the conventional ignition switch on the right of the steering column. Now wait for a couple of seconds as the ticking of the two fuel pumps slows, indicating that the fuel is up to the six twin-choke carbs. Give the accelerator pedal a couple of dabs to fill the Webers' float chambers and then turn the key one more click (preferably with the

Above: A Countach is not a car to jump into and simply drive away without a little consideration; it demands a period of warming up for both

engine and transmission from cold, and a gentle approach for the first few miles until everything has come to working temperatures.

clutch pedal depressed to lighten the load) to set the starter motor spinning.

With the injected US-specification engine, the dabs of throttle are unnecessary, but otherwise the procedure is the same.

For all its sophistication and big numbers, the Countach engine is completely untemperamental so long as it is carefully maintained – that means regular oil and filter changes every 5000 miles (7500km) and a full tune of ignition and carburation every 10,000 miles (15,000km).

In proper tune, it starts first time every time, requiring just a couple of gentle dabs on the throttle to clear all twelve throats and settle it into a steady, even tickover at around 1200rpm. At that speed it is totally undramatic, with a gentle whistling of pumps and drives and a slight intake hiss in spite of the big air filters and the bulkhead separating you from most of the action. It is mechanically quiet too, with little hint of the timing and valve gear noise that traditionally used to typify sporty V12s, just more of a low rustling of myriad parts working in unison. In the Anniversary Countach, even the burbling exhaust note is very subdued, buried behind additional cabin insulation, but that isn't the case with older cars, especially those with the optional 'sports' exhaust's raucous bark . . .

At this point, you may be raring to go, but the Countach isn't. Deep in the alloy and steel innards of its 5.2-litre V12, 3.9 gallons (17.5 litres) of cold oil and 3.7 gallons (17 litres) of cooling fluid are churning around; in the gearbox and final drive another 2.1 gallons (9.6 litres) of oil is beginning to circulate. It all needs warming to somewhere

Right: Although the Countach is both extremely low and extremely wide, and with that pitifully limited rear vision, it actually feels relatively

compact from inside. Big pantograph wiper sweeps the screen well enough, and flip-up lights retract neatly into tops of wings.

nearer its operating temperature, picking up heat from the motor as it grumbles into its stride. So sit for five minutes perhaps, keeping an eye on the water and oil temperature gauges and just allow everything to warm and settle gently. Let the clutch in once the engine is running, to let the gearbox warm too, and be patient.

CONTROL FEEL
Heavy metal
While you're waiting, familiarise yourself with the pattern of the five-speed gearchange sprouting from its slotted metal gate. It is a racing pattern rather than a 'conventional' five-speed saloon pattern; that means first gear is on its own, over to the far left and back, then a dog-leg shift right and forward to the second/third plane, and another shift across the width of the gate to fourth and fifth, completing the usual H-pattern. Reverse is straight ahead of first, but protected from inadvertent selection by a flick-down metal detente catch which with practice you can learn to flick out and change past in one smooth, rapid movement.

Now the Countach *is* ready to go, but maybe your own doubts are setting in. The clutch is extremely heavy (even though less so than on earlier Countachs) with a strange 'over-centre' feel near the top of its action; and the throttle has a long and progressive movement, but not until it has passed a disconcerting stiffness at the beginning of its travel which can make sensitive control of low speed trickling very difficult, especially when combined with the engine's almost rabid response to the slightest throttle movement.

What's more, the stubby gearchange might go almost directly into the 'box that it controls, but its movement at crawling speeds is heavy and difficult, and the effort needed to steer those big Pirelli tyres is similarly daunting.

These are things that you might soon find ways of overcoming – using a twisting ankle movement braced against the footwell side for first gingerly movements with the throttle, for instance; or using more thigh power than calf for the heavy clutch; or simply forcing the gearlever across its open gate until it lightens up as you get under way. But there's another problem too, and that is how much, or rather how little, you can see out of the Countach.

VISIBILITY
Good in parts
You only need to look at the car from outside to know that this is going to be a joke.

The good side is that forward visibility is superb, straight out to the road over the almost non-existent, steeply raked nose, seemingly almost to the point where you can feel your feet stretching practically between the two unseen front wheels.

The downside is that that is just about the *only* visibility you have. To the sides it is half decent (even with the small 'toll' windows interrupting half of the side panes) but in a car with the Countach's seriously stunted vertical growth, all you can usually see in traffic is the flanks of other cars or the wheel centres of very large trucks; that at least is how it feels in those first flushes of paranoia at driving something whose enormous

power matches its enormous price tag.

Then looking rearwards through the interior mirror you will see mostly engine cover in the letterbox-sized slit of the rear window, and mostly airscoops in the door mirrors, however you adjust them. That aspect is marginally better in injected cars and in the Anniversary model (which have slightly more friendly engine cover shapes), but is horrendously worse in any cars with the optional rear wing.

As for the small, angled, quarter windows behind the doors; well, forget those, all you will see there *is* the air boxes.

And the final problem is the way the Countach attracts attention to itself, *wherever* you go. That results in other drivers either tripping over themselves to get out of your way (even when you are parked) or being so desperate to have a closer look that their own driving goes completely to pieces. Pedestrians? Well, testing a Countach alongside a Miura SV, I once wrote: 'You can almost *watch* the fantasies forming as you drive the Countach through a crowded street...' I would still go along with that.

If you are wondering why you bothered and how to get out with more dignity than embarrassment, don't worry; it really isn't that bad.

Once you have overcome the sheer (and understandable) awe which the Countach engenders, you can begin to enjoy it for what it is: one of the most competent and refined high performance cars in the world.

THE COUNTACH PHILOSOPHY
Sympathy with commitment
Below the skin it is a completely different character from its 'bad-boy' sci-fi image. It certainly isn't a car for anyone without a serious commitment to driving; not a car (as Lamborghini always planned) for the merely dilettante *poseur*.

This is a car which *really* needs skill and understanding to bring out its awesome best. A car which needs a degree of aggression and decisiveness (based on ability, not bravado), tempered with sympathy for the superb design and engineering which created it.

In all honesty, perhaps the only people who will truly ever approach its phenomenal limits are the test drivers who live with it and constantly refine it, and a very, very limited number of owners who have the integrity to respect it and the skill to explore it. Any writer who can tell you the intimate subtleties of a car like the Countach on the strength of even a couple of weeks of cumulative experience in various examples is still really only scratching the surface – but perhaps even that is more than many owners will ever be tempted to do. The Countach is *that* exceptional.

The racing car feel never really disappears, but a lot of the intimidation does with familiarity.

With all the gauges up to working temperatures and pressures, you can begin to explore the car's capabilities. Strangely, the car can feel even more compact from inside than it looks from outside, even given the limits of visibility. Reversing is a problem, of course, but it is relatively easy to judge, instinctively, where the corners are, and how close you can come to kerbs and verges without clipping the expensive and vulnerable wheelrims. The low stance means that you don't

Left: Being so firmly sprung and damped, the Countach prefers smooth surfaces, but copes reasonably well with minor humps, bumps and potholes – although wide,
flat-treaded and square-shouldered tyres like the Countach's Pirellis tend to follow longitudinal marks like white lines and long ridges in the road surface.

get much chance to look over hedgerows and walls, and it's wise to remember that some higher vehicles like trucks and buses might not see *you* if you cut across their bows trying to beat the traffic.

The clutch, although heavy and with quite a short movement, takes up very smoothly, and the gearchange, while remaining baulky and difficult at low speeds, presents few problems in traffic once it has warmed up and once you have established the basic pattern. In this respect it is helped enormously by the flexibility of the engine, which will pull quite untemperamentally from less than 2000rpm all the way through to its maximum, even in top gear.

The one thing that really *does* give problems is the heavy, and therefore potentially jerky, initial throttle movement, but it gets better with practice. The brakes, on the other hand, feel reassuringly light and progressive; the pedal is absolutely rock solid, and the big, ventilated discs, once warm, stop the Countach positively but gently in stop–go traffic, while promising exceptional power at higher speeds.

As the car steadily warms, its character begins to show through. It is perfectly flexible and content to trickle around at very low revs in traffic, or just to rumble along through country lanes; and the ride comfort is extraordinarily good

for a car of this pedigree – coarse but only rarely jarring over mediocre surfaces at low speeds, and becoming progressively better as you drive more quickly. The wide, low-profile tyres are quite sensitive to surface changes if their shoulders pick up long marks like the edges of road repairs or even white lines, and there is a considerable amount of information pouring back from the front wheels via the steering, but it is positive information rather than unwanted jarring and the car feels totally free of unpleasant self-steering effects over bumps and ridges. It is also reassuringly immune to crosswinds and within a few miles, driven gently, it begins to feel almost mundane.

AWESOME POWER
What it's all really about

That feeling can be dispelled dramatically and instantaneously by exploiting the Countach's awesome power more fully. Just to recap on the numbers, current European-specification cars have 455bhp and 369lb ft of torque; and although the torque peak is at a relatively high 5200rpm, the spread is prodigious, anywhere from maybe 2000rpm onwards, with the torque and power curves crossing at around 4600rpm. As the typical *quattrovalvole*-engined Countach weighs only around 3300lb (1500kg), ready to roll, that output

(without which the car is not allowed to leave the factory) equates to a power to weight ratio of almost 310bhp per ton.

To put that into perspective, the Ferrari Testarossa has around 240bhp per ton, Aston Vantage Zagato around 266, and the Porsche 911 Turbo a mere 235. The roadgoing Countach is far closer to the limited edition, competition-oriented Porsche 959's 340bhp per ton, or the similarly esoteric Ferrari 288 GTO's 330 . . .

The power is prodigious, but in a relentless, gradually overwhelming way rather than with a snappy, difficult to control waywardness. As you ask it for more, the engine note changes from a dull, muted burble to the raw animal howl of a big, thoroughbred V12, and overlaid now with the characteristic top-end raspiness of the latest four-valve layout. The longitudinal layout and effective insulation mean that only some of the mechanical noise feeds back into the cockpit, but it is still magnificent, taking on a completely different, harder edge as you pass, say, 4500rpm.

Below: Cornering power of the Countach is awesome, not only because of size of the tyre footprint but also because of sophistication of all-round wishbone set-up.

Right: Latest generation P Zero asymmetric tread tyres have made the Countach even better in fast corners, not only for level of grip but also for feel and balance.

RESPONSIVENESS
The key to driveability

Perhaps even more impressive than the Countach's abundant power is its lightning responsiveness (no compromises of turbocharger lag here) both in picking up and in shutting down, with a feeling almost as though it has no flywheel effect at all, and no tendency to run out of revs.

Best of all is the way the Countach can translate that power into roadgoing acceleration and outright speed, such is the competence of its chassis and controls.

First, of course, the traction from the massive rear tyres, carrying around 55 per cent of the car's weight, is well up to coping with even this much power, and the combination of limited slip differential and the anti-squat geometry designed into the rear suspension keeps the drama of full-bore take-offs to an acceptable minimum.

Accelerating from rest, the thrust is sufficient to force you quite deep into the seats, but more impressive than that instant low-speed catapult effect is the unremitting way in which the surge carries on beyond 100mph, beyond even 150mph. More about actual figures later, but suffice it to say that the latest Countach will reach 60mph (97kph) comfortably inside of 5sec, 100mph (161kph) in just 10sec, and cover a standing start quarter-mile in less than 13sec and it is only just beginning. Where other cars may have hung onto the Countach until it has got into its mighty stride, they will eventually disappear in its mirrors when

the really big numbers appear.

Add to that the amazing flexibility which means this response and acceleration are available not just from a standstill but in any gear right across the speed range, and you will begin to get a hint, just a hint, of the Countach's colossal yet somehow subtle ability.

That sets the scene for most of the Countach's behaviour. It is immediately very confidence inspiring and user friendly – quite unlike the image it projects. And the harder you drive it, the better it gets. Once you're past that initial stiffness and on to higher speeds, the throttle sensitivity and heaviness cease to be a problem, and the gearchange becomes light and slick with familiarity, the flicks across the slots of the gate can be made as quickly as your hand will move, requiring just a positive movement that soon becomes delightfully second nature.

With the huge spread of torque there is less need to use the gearbox than in many cars, but you will undoubtedly use it just for the sheer aural pleasure of the V12's changing tune.

ROADHOLDING
Out of all normal realms

Driven fast but not towards its limits, the Countach begins to show the outstanding poise of its chassis and suspension. The front geometry was revised yet again for the 1988 model, the steering rack was relocated and the rear spring rates were changed, refining yet again the car's outstanding

basic layout. Remember that virtually the whole mass of the car is within the wheelbase – there is little of any consequence overhanging at either end; that makes for sharp, accurate handling, but as racing manufacturers who dabbled with this low-polar-moment configuration in the 1970s know, it also demands a high degree of skill to exploit its limits.

That is where the Countach is so good; the levels of grip from tyres of this size, controlled by such sophisticated suspension, are way out of the realms of ordinary experience, and the Pirelli P Zeros on the latest cars have taken that grip to yet another level; the works test drivers will tell you very positively that they are the biggest single advance on the Countach in many years. Their asymmetric pattern and dual compound tread give even more formidable roadholding through fast corners, even better dynamic balance, and the ability to put the Countach's power down even earlier coming out of any type of corner.

At all ordinary speeds, the Countach really *will* corner as if on rails; it will flatter an average driver by its massive ability to sprint between corners with its boundless but controllable power, will allow him to brake deep and late into bends without the nose diving into the road or the wheels scrabbling for grip, it will turn in precisely where the steering input tells it to and power away to the next curve, exploiting that unbeatable mixture of muscle and traction.

DEEP RESERVES
The rewards for real skill

Driven like this, at speeds which will already leave most cars trailing way behind, the Countach has huge reserves of ability. The more skill the driver can bring to the Countach, the more deeply the car

Left: Abundant power is of little consequence without adequate traction. Countach has plenty of both, and with some 55 per cent of its static weight distribution over massive rear tyre footprints can translate its 455bhp punch into quite staggering acceleration.

will let him explore those reserves.

And while the driver is reaching for the Countach's limits, the car will protect him from everything but sheer idiocy.

Early Countachs were prone to more understeer (the tendency for the front wheels to go straight on when pushed hard into a corner) than the testers thought ideal, but that was soon ironed out and the car's handling is now almost neutral up to very high limits indeed; it simply goes where you point it. The steering may be heavy at town speeds, but it lightens up beautifully when on the move, while still retaining all its sensitivity and feeding back delicate streams of information from the road. The suspension feels firm too, with very little travel, but a perfect balance of springing and damping rates. The ride soon loses its low speed jiggling and smooths out with speed, but it never becomes anything near floaty, always retaining that taut firmness of the near racer.

Now begin to push the Countach harder and you will discover more of its character. The braking power is simply staggering. There is no anti-lock system, but it is difficult in any case to lock the wheels with their huge tyre footprints, and the really experienced driver prefers the sensitivity of the conventional system. There is almost no nose dive under heavy braking, just as there is little squat under even the most violent acceleration, so the back end stays very firmly planted on the ground at all times. That has also removed any temptation to put too much braking bias to the front (which does tend to lead to premature wheel locking).

Enter a corner quickly and the steering weight builds up to tell you that the tyres are beginning to work harder, but there is virtually no body roll at all. A little quicker still and you will begin to feel the cautionary degree of understeer that is built in to warn of impending limits. If you ignore the warnings and keep the power hard on you will first push the nose even wider until you have to back off anyway. If you back off gently (not

suddenly), the understeer will check itself and the car will once again resume its neutral stance.

Only if you back off the throttle very sharply when you are going much too quickly into a corner will the car show any tendency to drift into gentle oversteer (where the rear wheels begin to step sideways) and you will need to correct with a delicate touch of opposite lock. But whatever you do, the car will respond completely progressively; there will always be ample warning that its attitude is changing and always ample control response to correct it. If you overstep the mark, it is more likely to be your fault than the Countach's . . .

Of course, if you choose to stay within bounds, you have the option of generating oversteer by exploiting the smooth walls of power which the engine can deliver, but confine it mainly to medium speed corners in lower gears – it is a very brave and very skilful driver indeed who pushes a Countach to its ultimate limits in the quickest corners; the car is simply better than most drivers. Be positive, aggressive even, but be circumspect – and remember that 455bhp.

BALANCE AND POISE
The underlying feeling

That said, the Countach *is* very protective; it has a wonderful feeling of balance and poise; and it simply never has the unpleasant tendency of the Miura to snap suddenly into oversteer without warning, for instance, or the feeling that it is taking charge. Its ability to communicate so lucidly what its chassis and tyres are doing at all times is what really makes its power and performance so usable.

It stays usable, too, right up to its formidable maximum. There is no more than the slightest

Below: Given enough space, acceleration will continue unabated until well over 150mph, although people will argue forever over the true maximum speed of a Countach. Even at these extremely high speeds, car's aerodynamic stability is superb, brakes reassuringly powerful.

hint of any aerodynamic lightness at extreme speeds. The steering lightens a little, but never to the extent where it suggests significant front-end lift. Even without the rear wing, the back is similarly stable and rooted to the ground, the only time it might feel even very slightly light is when braking on the absolute limit from very high speeds, but it warns rather than threatens. Cross winds have very little effect either, and with the big fuel tanks close to the centre of the car the handling balance changes very little on long journeys as fuel is consumed – probably at the rate of 10mpg (28.2l/100km) if you are exploiting the performance to anywhere near its limits.

PERFORMANCE
The million dollar question

Having said all that, it has to be admitted that it is still quite difficult to put definitive figures on that performance. That is partly because the factory have traditionally been reluctant to provide cars to be subjected to full, instrumented road tests, and partly because the number of places where the true maximum speed of a Countach can be recorded is very small indeed. Lamborghini's own quoted figures in the early days spoke of 'over 190mph', and that figure, or 186mph (that's around 300kph), has always retained some sort of mystical meaning for the Countach, even if no one

ever conclusively proved that the car would do it.

Probably the fastest reliable figures taken with proper methods and proper equipment come from a *Road & Track* magazine test in 1987 when they recorded an average of 179mph (287kph) at Volkswagen's test track, with a wingless, European-specification car. *Motor,* on the other hand, with a *quattrovalvole* car in 1985 couldn't beat 167mph

Below: The Countach in its element – fast open roads where the skilful driver can exploit both power and roadholding abilities. The car demands a positive approach, but tempered with respect. It will forgive most indiscretions, but abuse it and it will bite back. In reality it is better than most drivers need.

Above: Some 18 years after this stunning shape first drew cries of 'Countach!' from an impressed onlooker, it is still perhaps the most *evocative car in the world – and even as it approaches retirement it has lost none of its raw visual and mechanical impact.*

Below: Penultimate model, as in blue 1988 car, hinted at final changes, with slight softening of lines through the side strakes and other details *which the final Countach, the Anniversary model, took to a logical, neat, conclusion – nearer the clean simplicity of the original car.*

(268kph), even having removed the rear wing.

Other magazine tests have spoken of over 180mph (290kph) at the ultra-high-speed Nardo test track in southern Italy and *Fast Lane* reported a 190.1mph (305kph) two-way average in 1986, but that was against ordinary kilometre post markers on an Italian *autostrada* and timed with a hand-held stopwatch, so you can form your own ideas about how reliable that figure is in the light of other people's continued failure to match it. Or in the light of some of the works testers' admissions that the earlier, lighter cars were probably the fastest of all and that the Countach with all its later bodywork additions is about as aerodynamic as a barn.

It might also be said that *Fast Lane*'s results (giving the magazine full credit for their own integrity and ability with the watch) were achieved with a car from the works and a works test driver – and Lamborghini were well-known in the Miura days for having a few 'trick' engines on hand for impressing the right journalists . . .

As for acceleration, it's a struggle to find real agreement there either. *Fast Lane* reckoned on 0–60mph (97kph) in 4.2sec for their Countach, and 0–100mph (161kph) in exactly 10sec, where *Road & Track*'s best equivalents were 4.7 and 10.8. For what it's worth, Lamborghini's own claims for the *quattrovalvole* were a more modest 5sec to 60, with a quoted top speed of 185mph – or still hovering around that magical 300kph figure.

It is all fascinating, but also all largely academic for real road use. Any of the figures are pretty staggering by most yardsticks.

Better, perhaps, just to say that it is enough, that the Countach does whatever it does; and that after all these years it still has not only the aura of one of the greatest of supercars, but also the ability to back it up.

Whatever anyone else might throw at it, the Countach still ranks as perhaps the most exciting road driving experience of all.

THE FUTURE

By whatever name, the Countach philosophy looks set to survive

TEN YEARS AGO (or fifteen years ago, or even five years ago), very few people with any real interest in the motor industry would have given you odds that Lamborghini had a future of any kind. Until very recently, the cycle of one imposed crisis after another was more or less the story of Lamborghini's life. And without the Countach, Lamborghini probably *wouldn't* have made it to the end of the 1980s.

But they have made it, largely through a sheer will to survive, and the future now looks absolutely assured. What's more, the Countach ethos is still as strong a part of Lamborghini's plans as ever, with 1988's 25th Anniversary Countach marking the last use of the name, but the forthcoming Diablo being a clear cut promise to continue the line.

And what makes the future suddenly so bright is that Lamborghini finally have the substantial (and, more important, stable) backing that they have always desperately needed. It has come, finally, from the American car manufacturing giant, Chrysler.

CHRYSLER'S TAKEOVER
Stability at last
Chrysler's contacts with Sant'Agata began as long ago as 1985, when the two were tentatively discussing a joint sports car venture, just as Chrysler had also done with the Maserati company. Before long though, discussions changed from a simple collaboration to a major acquisition, and early in 1987 Chrysler concluded a deal whereby they effectively bought Lamborghini lock, stock and barrel – for somewhere in the 'bargain basement' region of $30 million.

It was no mere whim; in Lamborghini, Chrysler bought an outstanding asset, both for technological ability and for image, and Chrysler chairman Lee Iacocca was very quick to acknowledge the fact: 'We want to create in Sant'Agata our most advanced laboratory for top-end automotive engineering, taking advantage of Lamborghini's experience in the supercar market, and, in the future, also for development of the Formula One racing engine . . .

'No change of emphasis will be made to the general technical and philosophical line of Lamborghini products, and all the changes that may appear in the future will be carried out only if they are supported by valid technical reasons.

'The immense prestige gained by Lamborghini in all these years of technical excellence deserves this kind of respect . . .'

But as the president of Nuova Automobili Lamborghini, Emile Novaro, explains, Lamborghini have also retained the freedom to make most of their own decisions: 'Chrysler are shareholders, and, like all shareholders, Chrysler want a business plan. So Chrysler accept the plans, and then after that, Lamborghini are autonomous – but that doesn't mean that if we fall behind on our commitments they won't cut me dead just like they would anyone else . . .'

AFTER THE COUNTACH . . .
Going to the Diablo
At the end of 1988 there seemed little cause to worry that things should ever come to that; there was a great feeling of optimism and excitement at the factory, and the excitement was based on extensive plans for the future, not least for the Countach's successor.

Novaro explained how it slotted into the overall plan: 'Well, first of all, the factory at Sant'Agata will be expanded quite substantially. In 1982 we bought land behind the current works and to the side, so we now have the space to expand. From 1980 to 1987 we installed a great deal of new machinery in the existing factory and there was a lot of investment around 1985 and 1986 into the future.

'The Countach replacement will be the first new car we shall make. The idea now is that we will build approximately 500 of the 25th Anniversary Countach [which replaced the 5000 *quattrovalvole* in production in July 1988] and that will take us to the spring of 1990. And then the new car, the Diablo, will take over from the Countach.

'Of course, it is virtually finalised already – or at least if we are launching it in March 1990 I *hope* it is finalised! Everybody has their own feelings for the design, but sooner or later you have to make a choice, and that choice was made early in 1988 – because now, of course, we must make all the tooling to build the car.

'And it *will* be called Diablo. Some people say we are losing the strongest image we ever had by losing the name Countach, but then you know when we were building the Miura we had the same problem with introducing the name Countach! Any normal company has the same problem a lot more often than we do!

Left: *Emile Novaro, president of Lamborghini, has his finger firmly on the company's pulse. He has few doubts about its future state of health.*

Below: *Once thought to be the 'super-Countach' of the future, the experimental Evoluzione was finally sacrificed to crash-testing.*

Above: Impression of the next generation Countach. The name may have changed to Diablo, but the philosophy will remain the same – the ultimate *supercar; and in spite of Chrysler stamping their own identity, the shape is still very much the product of Marcello Gandini's genius.*

'I can tell you something; somebody very well known [it was Enzo Ferrari, in fact, but Lamborghini people don't often mention the name] when asked "what is your favourite car?" replied "it is the car that I haven't built yet" – and that is correct. If you live in the past you are dead.

'Of course, there is a risk, and certainly the Countach is a fantastic image, but we are Lamborghini, so we must respect exactly the same philosophy. The Diablo will be built by hand in exactly the same way as the Countach, with just the same sort of character, and the same chance for personalisation of individual cars.'

A NEW GENERATION
More power and sophistication
Even before Lamborghini released any details about the Diablo, known in the factory as project P132, there were clues to the direction they might be taking.

In 1985 they started a testing programme with what most people took to be a future 'super-Countach', which was more properly known as the *'Evoluzione'* – Countach-based but with lightweight carbon-fibre body panels and a remarkable 600bhp engine derived from the production V12. That car was used to test all kinds of systems, including a sophisticated four-wheel drive transmission, and it was finally sacrificed to crash-testing.

There were technical clues there to the next generation – like more power, more sophistication – and there are also clues in the 25th Anniversary Countach, which is the most refined, the most comfortable, the most habitable Countach to date.

The Diablo promises to be slightly longer than the current car, on a wheelbase probably as much as 6in. (152mm) longer – mainly for interior space, but also possibly for slightly more forgiving handling characteristics and ride comfort. Chrysler have made it clear that the Diablo will have to be more suited to US traffic conditions than the uncompromising Countach ever was. And build quality will be another major Chrysler priority.

But none of this is to suggest that with the Diablo the Countach image will be going soft; far from it. On the other side of the equation, the V12 will be uprated yet further, probably to a full 6 litres (366cu.in.) and at least 475bhp in European specification (maybe nearer 500bhp), leaving it clearly on top of the horsepower race once again.

A LIGHTER TOUCH
Saving weight with composites
What's more, by extending the use of lightweight materials which the Anniversary Countach had already started to exploit, the Diablo will be lighter than the existing car and more aerodynamic. The chassis will still be of the multi-tubular steel type, but using composite panels for reinforcement will allow it to be redesigned with some significant weight saving; and although the body will be mostly of alloy, as before, that too will have more composite panels, for both lightness and strength.

Under the skin, the possibilities stretching into the future are endless, but it seems that the Diablo will be launched with a conventional five-speed gearbox and two-wheel drive – with the promise of both four-wheel drive (possibly from as early as 1991) and an innovative electronically-controlled fully automatic transmission system also in the pipeline. And further extending the state-of-the-art thinking is the eventual possibility of 'active', that is fully computer controlled, suspension.

With that kind of specification, Lamborghini will be looking for a genuine top speed of more than 187mph (300kph) and probably closer to 200mph (320kph); in fact, early testing at the high-speed Nardo track in Italy confirmed that the latter figure was comfortably possible. To complete the performance picture, Lamborghini would expect a sub four-second 0–60mph time (0–97kph) to put the Diablo into the same sort of league as the limited edition Ferrari F40 and Porsche 959.

CHRYSLER AND THE DIABLO
'Italian soul, Italian temperament'
Finally, to clothe it all, Lamborghini and Chrysler had to come up with something in terms of body styling that at least continued the spectacular Countach tradition, and preferably improved on it.

It was not an easy task, and, although Marcello Gandini was the immediate first choice as stylist, the realities within a big organisation were by no means as simple as they were back in the early 1970s.

As Nuccio Bertone confirms, Lee Iacocca is another man who understands what he wants: 'From meetings with Iacocca I can see him as the sort of man who, like Ferruccio Lamborghini, has very clear objectives. I think we could immediately see ourselves as aiming for the same goal. And Iacocca for his part says that, yes, Chrysler now owns Lamborghini, but the cars Lamborghini must make must still have an Italian soul, and Italian temperament . . .'

Even Gandini, although it was rumoured for a long time that he did not like what had been done to his original ideas for the Diablo, can understand the Chrysler position: 'Of course, Chrysler have a lot of power over the people who work for them, and we have to accept that they probably do know more about their own market than outsiders do. And besides that, it is a mistake only to prepare cars that are similar to what went before – instead, the cars that we make now and all the cars we'll make in the future should be *different* from what went in the past; and not just Lamborghinis, all cars.

'It's not a secret any more that Lamborghini are building a new car to replace the Countach, but things are rather different now with the Chrysler backing. In the early days, the cars were always thought of as prototypes and so you could *always* think of doing something revolutionary in design terms. Part of the object was to get the newspapers to look and the people to talk. Usually there were just a few people working on any prototype and you could do all that with relatively little money. Now that has totally changed; with Chrysler involved there are far more people working on the car and there is a lot more money involved and that means a lot more risk.

'You can also say there is a lot more time to prepare a car; where a prototype was once made in two or three months there is now so much more time to think about ideas and drawings and changes; at the end it is much more difficult to produce something revolutionary simply because you are creating a car that is meant to go onto the market as soon it is introduced. Now, for instance, Chrysler asks for both practicality and comfort in the cars.

'But Americans still like the Countach because it is so exotic, and so European; so I think for the car to sell well in the USA it doesn't have to be designed in the USA . . .'

BERTONE SUMS UP
'In a word, the inspiration'
And in the end, it looks as though the stunning design for the Diablo will not be styled in the USA but *will* be very close to Gandini's original proposals, with its distinctive dipping waist line and an unmistakable family resemblance to the Countach. If that is the case, a lot of people will be very pleased, not least, perhaps, Ferruccio Lamborghini himself on his farms in Umbria.

The last word should go to Nuccio Bertone: 'Lamborghini history is really the result of courageous decisions by a courageous man, at a time when no one would have even believed he could have succeeded or survived with such plans. It was really a fascinating team of young people motivated by Ferruccio Lamborghini's personal charisma towards doing something that they felt was not so much a business as a destiny.'

In a word: 'Countach!'

INDEX

PICTURE CREDITS
The publishers wish to thank
the following photographers
and organisations who have
supplied photographs for this
book:

Author: 7 (top)

Autocar/Motor: 20 (bottom)

**Automobili Lamborghini
SpA:** 5, 6, 7 (bottom), 8
(bottom), 10 (bottom), 14
(bottom), 15, 16, 17 (top and
middle), 18, 20 (top), 21, 22
(top), 38 (bottom left), 39, 44
(cutaway), 45, 62

Carrozzeria Bertone SpA: 8
(left), 10 (top and middle), 11,
13, 14 (top), 19

**National Motor Museum
Photographic Library,
Beaulieu:** 23

Performance Car: 60, 61

Road & Track: 35 (cutaway)

All other photographs in this
book, including endpapers
and cover illustrations, were
taken by **Jim Forrest.**

The editor is also grateful to
Barbara and Roberta at
Lamborghini and to
Elisabetta Farmeschi at
Bertone. Their kind
assistance in helping to
arrange visits and meetings
and in supplying
photographs and translations
has been invaluable. Final
thanks go to Valentino
Balboni at Lamborghini for
his generous cooperation
and expert driving.